[handwritten inscription:] lay 05 to Sista Theola, Thanks for being on my Journey w/ me! I appreciate u. Shalom! Sista Linda

On Their Way to
WONDERFUL

A JOURNEY WITH NAOMI AND RUTH

Linda H. Hollies

THE PILGRIM PRESS
CLEVELAND

This book is dedicated to my company of supportive sisters of Woman to Woman Ministries, Inc.! It's especially for my personal agent, Jacqui Brodie-Davis, who believes in me! And Rev. Louisa Martin, who supplies me with daily "bytes" to keep me thinking and living large! I offer my grateful, loving, and appreciative thanks to Mattie Battles, Pattie Perry Finney, and all the women of the North Alabama United Methodist Women who allowed me to try this work on them at their Spiritual Formation Retreat. They opened my heart to additional multicultural love! They are truly my "sistas"! Thanks! To all my "over the years sistas" for hanging in with me on my journey! And to Mista Chuck, who is truly my Boaz!

The Pilgrim Press, 700 Prospect Avenue, Cleveland, Ohio 44115-1100
thepilgrimpress.com
© 2004 by Linda H. Hollies

For inclusivity and occasional clarity of meaning, the author has paraphrased selected scriptures. Scripture quotations, unless otherwise noted, are from the New Revised Standard Version of the Bible, © 1989 by the Division of Christian Education of the National Council of Churches of Christ in the United States of America and are used by permission.

Printed in the United States of America on acid-free paper

09   08   07   06   05   04   5   4   3   2   1

Library of Congress Cataloging-in-Publication Data

Hollies, Linda H..
    On their way to wonderful : a journey with Naomi and Ruth /
Linda H. Hollies.
        p.   cm.
    Includes bibliographical references.
    ISBN 0-8298-1604-6 (paperback)
    1. Ruth (Biblical figure).   2. Naomi (Biblical character).   3. African American women—Religious life.   4. Christian life—Biblical teaching.   5. Church year.   I. Title.

BS580.R8H65   2004
222'.3509505—dc22

                                                2004057296

CONTENTS

You were there when I needed you.

You stood above all of the others with your

strength and you guided me.

To each of you I offer my being,

my love and all that I am.

—Deidre Sarault

No trumpets sound when the

important decisions of our life are made.

Destiny is made known silently.

—Agnes DeMille

PREFACE

Once upon a time a man and woman fell in love under the wrong circumstances and at the wrong time. But they fell in love, as love is not a thing that can be predicted, arranged, or timed. Love happens when we least expect it. Their relationship began as a common friendship. Perhaps this is the way most long-term relations need to begin, but that's another story!

The man bought the woman a little heart of solid gold as a gift. It was a symbol of his deep and abiding affection. The woman cherished the little gold heart. The chain on which the heart was worn broke several times over the years. Nevertheless, that little gold heart remained a constant presence around her neck for over thirty years.

Finally, the couple married. The man gave her many other items of gold. Nothing ever replaced the value of that little solid gold heart. They had a family. Their lives were placed in the pressure cooker of time. Her children noticed her putting the heart in her mouth during times of stress and family crises. For the heart was a constant reminder of tangible love. Her friends noticed that she played with that little heart as she debated, argued, and wrestled with the situations of life. It was a reminder that love held her and even if the wrong decision was made, there was love to back her up every time she fell. The little heart whispered into her spirit the words of assurance that the man's love told her over the years. The little heart helped her make different decisions. They were not all the right decisions, but the little heart was used as a guide.

The woman tried hard to get her spouse to wear jewelry. He was a hard worker, a handyman, who was accustomed to working with his callused hands. After almost thirty years of marriage, he agreed to wear a new diamond ring for their anniversary. She was elated as she shopped for just the right ring. It had to be as special to him as the little heart was to her!

She finally found "the" ring! She gave it to him on a snowy Christmas Eve night. Knowing the love she had put into her search, he refused to take it off, not even to have it properly sized! Two days after Christmas he lost it! The search was intense. His pain was great. She refused to blame him or to finger point or to even say, "I told you so." He was hurt. She felt his pain.

The couple filed an insurance report and went in search of another ring. The ring had been purchased at an estate sale. There was not another one like it to be found! Finally, they found a ring almost like it. They settled for second best. This time it was sized before it left the store.

Circumstances dictated that the couple move from their home. They packed with care, hoping that the first ring would show up. It never did. And, to make matters twice as bad, the woman's gold chain got caught on a box she was unpacking, the chain broke, and her little heart was lost! She was bereft. She was terrified. What would she do without the "knowing" that the heart brought to help her solve her problems? How would she make decisions that were filled with his wisdom, if the little heart was not there to guide her?

It was really a horrible year for both of them. They were in a strange land. They were foreigners. They decided to go back "home," back to the same house they had left the year before.

In packing up for the return trip, they looked diligently for the little heart. It never showed up. Nevertheless, they packed with hope in their hearts. They had made a covenant years before: "Where you go, I will go, and where you lodge, I will lodge; your people shall be my people and your God my God" (Ruth 1:16). Both the man and the woman had aged. Both of them were beginning to tire of the packing and unpacking of a professional life. The man told the woman, "We're home. It's time for us to find ourselves." She agreed. She went to work to make this house their home again.

He took his callused hands and put them to work outside in the yard. He decided to sweep the curbside for it was filled with the debris of a long year of neglect. As he swept, he saw something shiny. He stooped to pick it up and discovered his lost ring! It had come off his finger as he had worked on their son's car on a snowy day. Though crushed, it had remained hidden in snow, under leaves and the collected junk that had been pushed closer to the curb by the street sweepers.

He found his source of tangible love from his wife! He didn't tell her a thing. He took the crushed ring to a jewelry store. They told him it could not be straightened. So, he took the stones from the crushed ring and one diamond stone from his replacement ring and had a little gold heart ring made for her. He then had the crushed gold melted down so that another solid gold heart could be made for her to place around her neck.

As you can imagine, after thirty years, his love for her had grown and her care of him dictated a bigger heart! He surprised her with the ring on one occasion and the solid gold heart on another. It's a love story worth telling as, over the years, this couple had shared loves, joys, sorrows, trials, and triumphs. They had gone through life's ups and downs. They had laughed and cried together. They had been lovers and friends. They had been each other's biggest cheerleaders. And, many times, they had been parents to one another.

The gold heart and diamond ring could never replace their love. And, even when these tangible gifts had been lost and had disappeared, their love kept them strong. They had made a covenant to stay together during good times and bad. Love held them. Love keeps them. Love holds them fast.

This is Mista' Chuck's and my thirty-plus years' love story! We continue to wear the tangible symbols of our love and give God thanks for this nonreplicable experience. It is our covenant of

Ruth to each other. It has held us through some very trying times. The book of Ruth is one of our favorite Bible stories, for it details our love.

BIBLICAL ROLE MODELS

In the deceptively simple narrative in the book of Ruth, a poor widowed foreigner becomes the wife of a respected man from Bethlehem and the great-grandmother of King David. Ruth is depicted as the ideal daughter-in-law, the wife and Gentile. For Naomi, she offers leadership, loyalty, and support associated less with daughters-in-law than with husbands. Her worth is proclaimed by the women of Bethlehem as being greater than that of seven sons.

In motivating Boaz, Naomi's Jewish relative, to action and in bearing his son, Ruth proves to be a worthy wife. Finally Ruth testifies to the contributions Gentiles can make to the covenant community. Through her leadership, loyalty, fortitude, and cleverness, she secures the future for herself, for her mother-in-law, and for the Davidic line. Yet, underlying these idealistic representations are complex social issues, gender relations, and personal motivations. The narratives focus on the lot of single women in rural Palestine and the problem of inter-ethnic marriages makes the book of Ruth substantially more than the unambiguous, pious idyll.[1]

There is nothing like a good love story. Love sells. This love story of two women, who are sista-friends, has stood the test of time. The book of Ruth is the love story of a Moabite woman who so strongly loved her Jewish mother-in-law that she risked leaving her homeland, her family, her religion's gods, and all that was familiar to her to walk into this wonderful Jesus story. It's the story of the two women's leadership abilities that saved their lives and extended the lineage of Jesus Christ in unthought-of and unheard-of ways.

This is the story of multicultural relationships. This is the story of womenfolk who were forced to learn new traditions, new customs, new ways, and new openness in order to live together and to survive. The first leader we find in this story is Naomi. She had left her home with a spouse and two children due to a famine in their native land. She had established a new home in a strange land. She had learned how to select, grow, prepare, and serve her family strange foods. She had been responsible for making a home among folks who were different, yes, even foreign to her in order to make their lives livable in a strange place with strange people.

This is a story of acceptance. In order for their family to survive and endure, Naomi and Elimelech had included strange women in their lives as wives for their two sons. "Back home" this would have never been tolerated. Back home these foreign women would have been called heathens and dogs! But the table had turned. The Jews were guests in a strange country. And if they wanted their family line to continue, they had to open their hearts, their minds, and their home to women who were totally unacceptable according to their faith traditions.

Jewish custom made Naomi responsible for teaching Ruth and Orpah how to be the best mates to their husbands. Jewish custom put Naomi in the leadership role as "lead" wife in their home. The men had the opportunity to work away from the home during the day, while Naomi was forced to spend time teaching the new "foreign" women. This story is not just about learning to sing in a strange land, but it's about learning how to mix and to merge two distinctly different cultures so that life might happen. It's obvious that Naomi took the lead.

The first principle of leadership is to *step up to the plate*. Life is not fair. Life is not easy. And famines are not usually planned! But when a famine in our life calls for change, we are shown by Naomi to step up and get ready to take a good swing. We have no mention of her grumbling, whining, or complaining during these difficult years. It's difficult, at best, when one couple marries and begins life on their own. However, under Naomi's leadership, we have three couples who had to live together and adjust to constant change. Life is interesting.

There is a Buddhist saying, "life is difficult," and that's a fair assessment, because in the midst of change and adjustment, Elimelech died. Naomi could not retire. She did not get a break. She could not take a leave of absence. As a widow, she was responsible for the living arrangements of the sons and their wives. The sons were responsible to make a living for all of them but Naomi was in charge of the home. Though she was a grieving widow the mantle of the household leadership did not pass from her to another.

The second principle of leadership is to *have a firm foundation and firmly stand upon it*. Each of us are in one of three places on the Ferris wheel of life. We are coming out of a life adjustment, entering a period of life adjustment, or a life adjustment is on its way! Change and adjustment will simply show up at our door. If we don't have a firm foundation upon which to stand, we will find ourselves blown away by the arriving storm. However, Naomi continued dealing with life due to her firm faith and trust in the provisions of the Almighty God.

I am sure that Naomi felt that this was the worst thing that could have ever happened to her. The lost of a spouse is one of life's greatest stress-producing factors. However, life was not finished with its adjustments for this mixed family. One son died. Then the other son died. It's hard to imagine this woman's grief. It's not easy to project myself into her story. For her pain's depth must have been unfathomable! Who wants to know the consequences of death that has snatched all of one's family? Who wants to exchange places with one who was feeling utterly alone, yet living with two foreign daughters-in-law under a custom that left her in charge?

It is clear that Naomi became depressed, filled with gloom and despair. It's not surprising that Naomi wanted eternal rest like her spouse and her sons. It's a fair assumption that she wished that she could have been taken instead of her sons. But life does not ask our opinion! Life just waits for our response. Leader that she was, Naomi had the answer.

Principle number three is to *make sure decisions*. We do not have a lifetime guarantee that the decisions we make will get us the results that we want. Scripture declares that wisdom is found in the counsel of two or three. It does not seem that Naomi had that wisdom available to her in Moab. So, when there was no counsel to seek, what might she do? Naomi made the decision to return to the place of her beginnings. This is wisdom. If life leads you in circles and you cannot figure out which way to go, always return to the place where you started and begin again. Since she and her family had left Bethlehem due to a famine, the Ferris wheel of life had turned many times. The famine had now come to Moab. It was time to go back to the place of the first principle!

Naomi led the way out of Moab and the two daughters-in-law followed her to the crossroads. She led them to the place where she gave up her position as head of the family. She led them to the place of challenge. She led them to their own place of decision. She shared with these two women her best wisdom and then gave them her sage advice, "Go back home to your first family!" Sometimes, the best place to go when failure seems everywhere is home. Sometimes we need the nurture, the cushion, and the respite of home. Sometimes we need a place with people who will allow us to stop, chill, think, assess, and then strike out again fresh. Naomi did not relinquish her leadership qualities. She allowed two women the freedom of choice. Naomi introduced them to the act of liberation. Naomi permitted them the full power of walking into their own divine destiny. She led them with her actions and her words: "Go home!"

CHOICES

The words we hear in many marriage ceremonies, to keep God in the center of their relationship, come from this story of loving commitment. Two women were standing at the crossroads of life. Naomi, the older Jewish woman, had lost all she had while living in Moab. Years before, she, along with her husband Elimelech and their two sons, had left Bethlehem, which means city of bread, on a journey seeking bread for their survival.

While in Moab, her two sons, Mahlon and Chilion, married Moabite women, Ruth and Orpah. Misfortune struck this home, as all three males died without leaving a male offspring! The three widows were bereft and without support. And, to further complicate their already bad situation, famine struck Moab.

Naomi, bitter, decided to return to Jerusalem and die. She and her daughters-in-law began the journey together. Only one made a covenant to walk with her, take care of her, and provide a shoulder to lean on for strength. This is her story of covenant love. The book of Ruth is a worthy read. Ruth, the foreign woman, decided to be like that diamond ring. She twinkled! Love does that for you.

The covenant, found in Ruth 1:16–17, reads:

Do not press me to leave you
or to turn back from following you!
Where you go, I will go; where you lodge, I will lodge;
your people shall be my people,
and your God, my God.
Where you die, I will die—
there will I be buried.
May the Lord do thus and so to me,
and more as well, if even death parts me from you.

Ruth and Esther are the only two books in the Holy Bible named after women. Both of these books continue to be read during yearly Jewish holy days. Ruth is read during the celebration of the spring harvest festival, Shabuoth, or during the Christian Pentecost. Esther is read during Purim.

Both of these stories of celebrated women deal with similar issues of being foreigners to those in power. Family devotion and loyalty are other central themes carried through both stories. Neither book speaks directly about God, but both detail God's providential care of those outside of the power circles. And both of these books detail the bodacious acts of ordinary women who dared to risk their lives without the protection of male figures.

Authorship of Ruth is not known, but it's set in the period of the Judges, which pulls in another powerful woman, Deborah. This was a period of spiritual decline in Israel. Throughout the book of Judges, it is repeated that "the people did what was right in their own eyes" (Judg. 21:25). So their continued faith in God's provision, the moral standards and covenant relationships, are the issues brought to bear in the Book of Ruth. The story, which begins with three women involved in a set of complex social issues, levirate marriage customs, and the loss of "wonderful" in their lives, makes it our story to explore!

Ruth became part of the genealogy of Jesus as outlined in the first chapter of Matthew. Ruth, a foreign woman, found herself a mother of the Davidic kingly line that leads to Jesus Christ. Ruth walked with Naomi from an empty place in Moab to a place of fullness in Bethlehem. Their journey from poverty to plenitude due to their loving-kindness is one that pulls us into the story and teaches us lessons that will serve us well. This is the journey from hell to "Wonderful"! And, it begins with one quality decision.

ACKNOWLEDGMENT

My biological sister, Riene Adams-Morris, is facing a life-threatening disease. It has changed all of our lives. One day, the four "Adams girls" together fasted and prayed as we sought to help Riene "see and give" more positive responses to her situation. I suggested, big sister that I am, that she respond to health inquiries with, "I'm on my way to Wonderful." Thus was born the title of this book. None of us know where our journey will lead. We are all following the guidance of The One who alone, knows and directs our steps. But eventually we discover Wonderful on every journey. The promise is, "I know the plans that I have for you. Plans for your good." That's Wonderful!

I give God great thanks for the sista talks that I can have with three women who know me best and love me just the same: Jacqueline Donna Adams-Brodie-Davis, Riene Cornelia Adams-Morris and Regina Camella Adams-Pleasant. We are each on this journey with Riene, and now with you as we travel to Wonderful!

INTRODUCTION

HAVE YOU LOST YOUR MIND?

The question comes when you have done something ludicrous. The question comes when you have done something out of the ordinary. The question comes when you have done something that others feel is out of the box, over the line, and beyond their reasoning. My Mama used to ask me this question when I had gone beyond the limits she thought I knew! "Miss, have you lost your mind?"

"Have you lost your mind?" is a question that was to make us stop and think. "Have you lost your mind?" questioned our ability to follow the common and ordinary practices of others. "Have you lost your mind?" was one of the ways that others tried to reign in those of us who dared to go beyond the status quo and the socially acceptable. So, I ask through this book, "Have you lost your mind?"

It is my prayer that you answer, "Yes!" The old mind that we were born with is contrary to the mind of God. The old mind that we were born with wants to go along with the crowd, fit in, and get along. I stay in trouble because I lost my mind when I accepted Christ as my personal Savior. I cannot fit in with the status quo because I now have the mind of Christ. I am the one who thought it was not robbery to act like a child of the Most High God and, with power, create in my tongue. It finally dawned on me that I had lost my old mind!

Now, I never answered, "Yes 'Ma'am" to Mama, because that was asking for a slap dead in my mouth! I earned a couple of those and didn't like the experience. But Mama is gone to glory now and I can confess before the world that my old mind is gone, washed away, regenerated, and born again! I have a mind today that calls me, summons me, and demands of me to be bodacious, powerful, and creative, and to think outside of the world's narrow boxes.

Having a new and improved mind also calls me to run away from evil and to run to embrace Wonderful. That is not the logical sequence of the old mind that I had. My old mind was filled with the *seven things that God hates*. Hate is a strong word. Hate is a nasty word. Hate is a dirty word. Yet, there are seven things outlined in Proverbs 6:16–19 that even God hates, detests, and finds despicable!

God hates our pride and arrogance. The old mind said, "I can do this by myself." Or, as we have heard, "We can pull ourselves up by our own bootstraps." But the new mind says, "Without God I am nothing, and with God there is nothing that can't be done!"

God hates a lying tongue. The old mind said, "Tell a lie for peace's sake." The new mind says, "Confront evil with a word fitly spoken." Always remember Ananias, who lied to the Church about how much money he had received for selling his property and fell dead in front of them. Along comes his silly wife, Sapphira, who goes along with his lie and also falls dead. Read the story in Acts 5:1–11 and see for yourself what a "peace sake's lie" can earn.

God hates hands that shed innocent blood. The old mind is what is allowing drive-by shootings in our neighborhoods to occur—occurrences that are no different and no better than the former night visits of the Klan that we detested. The new mind of Christ helps us to keep in check our old mind's tendencies toward the violence in each of us! Yes! I mean you too!

God hates a heart that devises wicked schemes and evil thoughts. Martin Luther, the Church reformer, said that, while we can't keep eagles from soaring above our heads, we can keep them from building nests in our hair. Those who devise wicked schemes not only permit, but also encourage the eagles of sin to build nests in their hair. Our new mind calls us to love, and to love, and to love again.

God hates feet that are quick to rush to evil. And, without a doubt, our old mind allows us to keep the mess going! Say "Amen," somebody! The new mind calls us to the ministry of forgiveness and reconciliation at every juncture. We are now ministers of reconciliation with a divine mission to work through our mess and to help others to get through theirs.

God hates a false or lying witness, who pours out lies. The old mind loves to spread gossip. The old mind loves to pull people down. And the old mind enjoys hearing "the dirt" on others. But the new mind refuses to engage in these practices, for the Holy Spirit calls us to build each other up, to encourage the weak among us, and to warn those who come to bring us juicy backbiting news. Got a new mind?

God hates one who sows discord. We cannot remain in cliques, groups and cells of dissension and division when we get a new mind. We cannot be on the bandwagon of beating up leaders, pulling down brothers and sisters when we loose our old mind and gain the mind of Christ. We cannot be among the best hell raisers, the most noted sharp-tongued critic or the best source of bad news when Jesus comes and brings us a new mind. The old has passed away; behold, the new has come!

Mama would ask me if I had lost my mind when she felt that I had forsaken the wisdom she had imparted to me. Mama would ask me if I had lost my mind when I did something that would bring shame and embarrassment upon our family's name. Mama would ask me if I had lost my mind when I did something that was beneath her expectations of my behavior. Mama's questioning was enough for me to get a clue that I'd better not be found doing or saying whatever it was that she had questioned. Her punishment was swift and sure. So is God's!

Have we lost our good sense? Paul Harvey observed on one of his radio programs that "the world is jiving us. We call pornographic pictures art. We build shrines to Elvis. We get our truth

3

from tabloids and our religion from Shirley MacLaine."[1] This is a book seeking to help us to lose the old mind that we were born with and to receive the new mind of Christ. For with this new mind we can go through the mess of our lives in victory. We can anticipate the miracle that comes after the mess, for when we have a new mind, we will know where we get our source of Truth!

Do you stop and think about your words? Do you pause and consider your behavior? Have you stopped to think that you are living your eulogy? Unless we honestly and sincerely repent of having lived out of the old mind set, until we confess that we need to lose our old mind and be born again, regenerated and transformed by receiving a new and godly mind, we will live any sort of way and miss our destiny within the realm of God.

A local newspaper religion editor recently wrote an article detailing how European American, mainline Protestant preachers are primarily avoiding the use of the term "hell." The word is offensive. The word is archaic. The word disturbs. The word is from another more hostile arena of thought. Well, all of that is true. However, it's not the whole truth. Unless we lose our old minds and refrain from the old way of living, in hell we will lift up our eyes!

The Bible talks about a hell that is hot and tormenting. I believe that. And even if hell is ice cold and a place to chill, I just believe there is such a place for those who live in the mindset that God hates. So, I am busy trying to lose my old mind. The new one that comes from Christ is an improved model, and it's ours for the asking.

OUR SEASONS WILL CHANGE

Come and take a journey with me, as we use Naomi and Ruth as our key role models of women in Scripture who found themselves in messy situations. Instead of using "normal and conventional" wisdom, they lost their minds and did the new, different, and never tried. They made the pages of the Holy Writ! They can teach us something about walking through the messes that we find ourselves in on a daily basis. It's obvious that the old, tried ways are not working for most of us. So, we have little to risk as we seek to lose our minds and discover the mind of Christ, who was and is the ultimate victor over messy situations!

Ruth and Naomi will walk us through the seasons of the Christian year as we journey toward our divine destiny. They will point us toward the signs of each season and provide us with maps for checking our own trip. The Christian year begins with Advent, that pregnant season that prepares us for the splendor of Christmas and new birth. Both Ruth and Naomi show us how to navigate the advent of new choices in our lives.

Christmas is not one single day! The season of Christmas, where we give birth to new selves, leads us into Epiphany, where those who are wise will offer their innermost treasures unto the Christ in us. Epiphany leads us into Ash Wednesday and the penitential season of Lent. Lent is our individual and corporate preparation for celebrating the death, burial, and resurrection of Jesus Christ. We are then ready for the season of Easter that carries us into the season of ordinary time, where without fanfare and festivals we will live the abundant life knowing that another season is headed our way.

The seasons of our lives come to remind us of God's faithfulness. If you really want to comprehend the questions that God is asking of you along the Christian journey, check out the season that you are walking through. Seasons come. Seasons pass. We cannot stay in one season and settle down for good. Each season brings us change. Each season offers us growth and further personal development. Each season has both its gifts and its required pain. Each season comes with its distinct colors, flavors, beauty, and death. For every season must die in order for the new season to come forth in fullness. The exploration of the Christian seasons will provide us with more information, inspiration, and motivation as we journey toward the land of Wonderful and the potential of our divine destiny.

It's good to have you along as we explore and learn from Naomi and Ruth. I anticipate that we will learn many new truths and methods in the days ahead. For these women will release unto us ancient wisdom that will work for us if we allow it. This book did not just come to me one day. This book was birthed in me at a challenge from my sista-friend, Pastor Constance Wilkerson.

Connie called and said that the Victorious Christian Women's Conference had a workshop with my name on it: "It Looks Like

Failure, but It's Only a Stepping Stone." I didn't want to do it because when she called, I was in one of my "looking like failure" situations! And I didn't want to reflect upon it. I just wanted it to hurry and be done. However, God demands that I personally learn the lessons that I teach! So, in my prayer time, I began to seek answers from God about "my" biblical models for getting to "my" stepping stones to wonderful! Ruth and Naomi came to my house and we have spent many days together!

I urge you to come along and not turn your back on a very pregnant future. I'm ready to begin the journey, on my way to Wonderful. How about you?

A CONTEMPORARY RUTH

In her book, *10 Bad Choices that Ruin Black Women's Lives,* Dr. Grace Cornish details the Ten Commitments for women on the journey to Wonderful. She developed these rules as a psychologist, businesswoman, and writer. To see exactly what Grace has said, buy and read her book. She offers us valuable insights.

The journey to Wonderful requires, yes, even demands many life altering behaviors. My dear beloved sista-friend, you are so important to me. I need you in order for us to both survive and to make a lasting difference in our assigned places in the world!

LET'S PAUSE AND BREATHE

Wonderful is a journey. Wonderful is a trip. Wonderful is a process. Where is Wonderful for you? What is your passion? What will it take for your journey to Wonderful?

What "commitment" speaks most loudly to you today and makes you go, "Hummmm?"

_____

_____

_____

_____

Thank God for girlfriends! Who else would try so hard to keep our secrets, laugh hysterically at our silly jokes, wipe our tears after yet after another breakup, take us out to celebrate our engagement (or divorce for that matter), and stand by our side as we make our way through all the trials and tribulations that life has to offer? Only a true friend. Girlfriends!

—Chrisena Coleman, *Just Between Girlfriends*

ONE

THE SEASON OF ADVENT

WONDERFUL IS A STATE OF GRACE

"Don't urge me to leave you"

The journey to Wonderful requires a commitment to walk with others in community, for a key principle of leadership is how to build and to work with a team. The road to our destiny is filled with too many traps, detours, and pitfalls for us to try and make it on our own. We all need others who are willing to assist us in meeting the team objectives and goals.

Naomi had played solo for so long that the idea of a team was foreign to her. Naomi was determined that she would make the trip back to Bethlehem on her own. By this time, she did not think of herself as a superstar, just as one left all alone. With her spouse and her sons dead, it seemed as if life had snatched all her teammates and left her alone. She was on her way to Bethlehem. And she would make it on her own, thank you very much!

Mrs. Dorothy Height, president emeritus of the League of Negro Women, puts our plight in life like this: "Women of color have never done what they wanted to do. They always do what they have to do." This was Naomi's determination that day at the cross-roads. She was not accustomed to help or assistance. She was not familiar with the concept of "Let's think this through together." And, being a woman, she had no place within her thought process of a "helpmate"! She had always met life on a playing field that was unfair to women and she had done what was necessary for life. This trip home was not going to be any different. Or so she thought.

Bethlehem, which means "city of bread," was Naomi's birthplace. She and her spouse, Elimelech, had moved into Moab years prior when a famine hit their homeland. But life had not been nice to Naomi. Not only had her husband died, but her two sons had grown up, married Moabite women, and died, leaving them in her care!

Now, there was famine in Moab and Naomi determined to go back to Bethlehem, bitter and alone. The laws of Israel made Naomi responsible for her two daughters-in-laws, Ruth and Orpah. They were obligated by the levirate system of belonging forever to the family into which they had married. Can you imagine being forced to marry the brothers of your spouse or significant other? Does it make your stomach turn when you recall how many of them look, act, think, and behave? Well, Ruth and Orpah and any woman married into a Jewish family had to deal with this scary reality. This was the ruling of the levirate system. You were in the family until your death!

Therefore, by Jewish law these Moabite women were to remain with Naomi until either she remarried and had other sons that would marry them or until they could find a close relative to Elimelech to marry them. However, these two women were not Jews. They belonged to the land of Moab. So, in good leadership style, Naomi gave them both a chance at a different life.

Naomi was caught between a rock and a hard spot. She was too bitter to remarry. She was too old to have other sons. She was too tired to imagine a future where she and two other widows would find provisions. So, standing at the crossroads, she urged both women to return to their parents' homes. Like many of us Naomi was trapped into feeling that, without men in our lives, it was all over. She said that their only hope was to find other men and produce sons to care for them. She felt cursed by God and empty even of hope! Wonderful for her had become history!

It was time for a decision. It was time to make a new choice. It was the season of Advent for these three women. Advent is the Christian Church's season of preparation for the birth of Jesus Christ. This also means that during Advent, Mary, his mother, is pregnant! Advent means that the Church universal is moaning, groaning, throwing up, confused, and perplexed, asking, like Naomi, "How can this be?" Advent is the season when we look at our lives and try to clean up and clear out the old "stuff" that prevents us from saying, "There is room in this inn for Jesus Christ."

Naomi knew that a change had come for her. She was preparing for death! She wanted a quiet and uneventful season. She wanted to go back home and die in the comforts of the familiar. She wanted to go back to her native land where the customs were not strange and the foods were recognizable. So she changed her name to Mara. She named herself "bitter." She was angry at God. She was disappointed with life. She felt that a period had been put at the end of her life. She was ready to go home and give birth to her death! To Naomi, death seemed like all the grace that God had to offer her.

In clinical terms, Naomi was depressed. Women of color have been told, taught, and socialized to believe that depression is a "whites only" state of being. "A 1996 survey conducted by the National Mental Health Association found that African Americans are confused about the definition, causes, and symptoms of depression.

- Sixty-three percent of us think depression is a personal weakness. *Depression is not a personal weakness; it is a treatable mental illness.*

- Only thirty-one percent of us think depression is a health problem. *Depression and other mental disorders are health problems.*

- Fifty-nine percent of us think it is normal for a woman to be depressed during menopause. *Depression is not normal at any stage of life.*

- Forty-five percent believe it is normal for a mother to feel depressed for at least two weeks after having a baby. *Many mothers may experience a few days of baby blues after giving birth, but depression that lasts for two weeks or more is not a normal part of childbirth.*

- Forty-two percent believe it is normal for someone to be depressed for more than a year after the death of a spouse. *Feeling lonely, lost, and sad is a part of the grieving process. But depression that lasts more than six months after the loss of a loved one is not normal.*

Myths like these keep us from recognizing depression and getting the treatment that we need. This makes it hard for us to support our loved ones who are suffering from depression or to ask for help when we need it. Depression is common, but it is not normal. No one wants to be depressed, and no one should have to just "live with it."[1]

Thank God that women of color are beginning to recognize when they feel like Naomi and know that they have a variety of options to choose from in order to walk through it as opposed to trying to walk the journey all alone. For the reality is that we all come to these crossroads. We all have to decide what our name will be in the future. We all are forced to make life-changing decisions.

Naomi told her daughters-in-law: "'Go back each of you to your mother's house. May the Lord deal kindly with you, as you have dealt with the dead and with me. The Lord grant that you may find security, each of you in the house of your husband.' Then she kissed them, and they wept aloud" (Ruth 1:8–9).

Girlfriend had it all figured out. It's obvious she spent much time deciding how each one's life should be lived out in the future. It was her job to be the lead woman in her home. This was her position of authority. Her best wisdom said, "Send these women back to their own mothers." Isn't it just like us to only see what's in front of our face? Isn't this our usual stance of getting stuck in a bad situation and deciding that it is "the end?" Without consultation, without counsel, and without the other two women's consideration, Naomi made decisions for all of them!

In many ways Naomi's decision was a good one. In several ways Naomi was working toward a quality decision like the effective leader that she was. For the time does come when a woman must decide to give birth to herself! A woman is forced to say, "No!" to others in order to say, "Yes!" to her own self.

Quality leadership demands that we all take the time to be *first* on our list. Quality leadership demands that we spend time by ourselves, with ourselves, and for ourselves. There must be time factored in for devotion and prayer. There has to be a scheduled appointment for a spa day, nails, and pedicures. There must be time where we invest in our own souls, plant in our own gardens, and till the soil of our own being. Without the "me time" that is required, we will try to lead others out of a bankrupt inventory! No leader can lead without stopping to replenish. And women need to take more time alone because they dare to give more of themselves away!

Naomi was locking up her bra! She was too tired to allow any others to suck up her energies. She was determined that one was a whole number. The only thing she forgot to figure into her equation was that, in Advent, all of us are pregnant!

A PREGNANT SEASON

In the season of Advent there is a quiet mystery moving about in the world. In Advent, a quiet and reflective season, God is not resting, but working in mysterious ways, weaving and wondering how we will respond to what appear to be dead situations in our life. A third-century mystic, Meister Eckhart, asked the question, "What does God do all day?" He answered his own question. "God sits on a maternity bed, birthing thoughts, visions, and ideas!" We all have the potential, the opportunity, and the ability to be available to pregnancy by God.

Good leadership skills are honed in the quiet time of Advent. Good leaders learn how to take the time to be still and allow God to drop some of those "birthing thoughts, visions, and ideas" into their spirits. For when God is the co-parent, we never have to worry about "child-care" for our "new infant!"

We go to school. We read the latest leadership guides. We practice quality leadership models. We do continuing education to make sure that we are well informed. Then, we put all of our education and information upon the altar of our hearts and allow God to move in our spirit, directing how and where we are to go next and with whom we are to work.

Just as on the very first day of creation God stepped out into the deep midnight, pushed away the boundaries of otherness, and made way for everything new, Advent comes. Advent comes to break into our everyday routines, stir up our lives, make us sit up and take notice that change has arrived! We are not the same. We are not even who we were yesterday. We don't know who we will be tomorrow. But at the crossroads we have to choose new directions. We cannot be a "little bit" pregnant! Since we have not aborted or miscarried the seed of "perhaps" that is growing within us, we will not allow anyone to stop our journey toward our destiny into Wonderful.

The day before, Ruth and Orpah had awakened as widows in the home of their mother-in-law. They were her dependents. The three women were without male provision. There was no welfare system. There were no governmental agencies to offer them assistance. Life for them seemed bleak. But they were together and there was hope in the air. "For surely I know the plans I have for you, says the Lord, plans for your welfare and not for harm, to give you a future with hope" (Jer. 29:11). However, Naomi had made a decision that would have rocked the whole boat! Thank God that all three women came to the crossroads together.

Orpah allowed Naomi to persuade her to return to her mother. With a few words of encouragement, Orpah kissed her mother-in-law good-bye (Ruth 1:14). And, with this one kiss, Orpah walks out of biblical history. We hear nothing else about her. She walks backwards and leaves us all wondering how her story ended. Not only did she kiss her mother-in-law good-bye, she kissed off her destiny as part of a greater scheme that had already been planned. She walked out on the season of her Advent! She allowed her pregnancy to be stillborn!

The admonition to walk away, to turn around, and to leave her season of expectancy did not turn Ruth around. Naomi's plan was not her plan. With marriage to a "foreign" family she had already made a decision to become a risk taker. She had already made herself vulnerable. Now she offered the gift of her youth, willingness to work, and a sense of value and self-confidence to her mother-in-law. Instead of allowing Naomi to go it alone, Ruth "clung" to her.

"Ruth assumes the closest physical position a woman takes to another in scriptures. The Hebrew word for clung is *dabaq*. This word echoes the ideal marital relationship expressed in Genesis 2:24. The text's further uses of *dabaq* continue to focus on relationships between women. Boaz and Naomi both urge Ruth to "*dabaq*" or cling to the women in the fields (Ruth 2:8, 21). It means to stay close or to keep close. For it is in the company of women that Ruth, like Naomi, will find safety."[2] Naomi did not quite "get it," but Ruth was offering to shelter her from the storms of life, to stick by her side without fail, and to be her protection from harm and starvation.

Naomi did not "deserve" the grace offered by Ruth. She could never have bought, earned, or demanded this gracious favor being offered by a woman who had been "foreign" to her. But when you are a gift, you must prepare yourself to receive undeserved gifts in response. "Give, and it will be given to you. A good measure, pressed down, shaken together, running over, will be put into your lap . . ." (Luke 6:38). Most of us are not taught how to be gracious when it's time for us to receive. It is against our theological training to allow others to tend to, nurture, or care for us! We know well how to give to, tend to, and nurture others, even at our own detriment. But Advent is leading us to the Christmas season where we are to both give and to receive gifts.

Naomi thought, "One down and one to go!" She told Ruth, "See, your sister-in-law has gone back to her people and to her gods; return after your sister-in-law" (Ruth 1:15). That's so much like a woman who encourages us to pay attention to the status quo. Isn't that what we, those who have sisters, heard as younger women, "Why don't you behave like your sister? She's a nice girl."

As young women, we knew then that we were not "nice" in the normal and customary manner. We knew that we had big dreams inside of us. Way down on the inside, we felt the tug to explore the different. We sensed that there was more to life than being a "nice" girl who went along in order to get along! We wanted to try to enlarge our territory. We wanted increase in our life. We had a desire to expand our boundaries. We liked a bit of commotion and even drama. There seemed to be more to life than what we saw from our mothers, their mothers, and our big sisters. We wanted more! Ordinary was never good enough for us. We wanted Wonderful!

In her autobiography *Dust Tracks on a Road*, writer Zora Neale Hurston puts it this way: "One of the most serious objections to me was that having nothing, I still did not know how to be humble. A child in my place ought to realize I was lucky to have a roof over my head and anything to eat at all. And, from their point of view, they were right. From mine, my stomach pains were the least of my sufferings. I wanted what they could not conceive of."[3]

Ruth wanted more than what she had already experienced. She knew what was behind her. She knew that there was a famine behind her. She knew that the gods of her land had not provided food or husband. She realized that there was little saying "life" to her back there. So she told Naomi, "Do not press me to leave you . . ." (Ruth 1:16). Her leadership skills kicked in and became primary. She was finished being a dependent. She was going to take the authority and make the necessary decisions. She had been a faithful part of Naomi's team and had a good sense of what was required to lead a family towards survival. Ruth was willing to do the difficult and seemingly impossible tasks of making something happen on the journey.

Ruth recognized that she had to leave the old in order to embrace the new and different. The disease of "dat'll do" is terminal! The ability to remain in what you know is a place of famine, desolation, and approaching death is not wisdom but foolishness to the maximum! To realize that there is more for your life and yet remain "stuck" as you fantasize that things will get better is a living hell. In order to get out of a dead situation we have to first decide that there is more somewhere else. We are not required to know all the specifics. We just need to wake up to the reality that there is more.

Ruth was willing to go forward and she refused to allow another woman to deter or delay her journey toward her destiny.

This was a new season. She felt the stirring within. She trusted that Naomi's God would make provision for both of them since she was a willing worker. She was pregnant with leadership. It was Advent in her life. A place called Wonderful was ahead. She took off stepping along. "Come on, Mother, Wonderful is this way!"

A CONTEMPORARY RUTH

Twenty years ago, she was a young woman with aspirations to be an ordained clergy woman. But she was both black and Baptist. Being female, these were huge odds to go up against. Women in the Baptist Church, both black and white, knew their place and pretty much were stuck in "dat'll do" positions, low on the totem poles. But Suzan (Sujay) Johnson-Cook was not satisfied with being a "missionary" or a licensed evangelist. She wanted to be a pastor. She knew that the God of Advent had impregnated her with a big dream.

Sujay graduated from school and went on to college, where she majored in communications. Her parents continued to tell her that she had to make a living, even while dreaming! Sujay knew that preaching was a form of communicating good news to people everywhere. So she invested herself in studies and decided to go to seminary. People thought she was crazy, for she was a bright student with a great future ahead, if she only knew her place!

When you meet Sujay you are attracted to her big and beautiful smile. She was the proverbial "nice girl." She did the right things. She said the correct things. And she showed up in the wrong places according to the dictates of the black, male-dominated Baptist Church. But she and God had a thing going. She was pregnant and she was not a single parent with this vision of Wonderful. She had spent time listening to God and agreeing to go a different route than the "average" nice, black Baptist church woman.

She registered and attended the Hampton Minister's and Musician's Guild in Hampton, Virginia. No woman had ever been allowed to stand upon the platform; it was surely the "good old boys'" place. Sujay's winning smile and quiet listening manner allowed her to remain in places that most women found too hostile.

She sat in the midst of the "big boys" with dignity and a calm assurance that she would find bread in this place.

The Conference refused to allow women to even gather on the grounds for a luncheon to talk about ministry! Although it is touted as an interdenominational event, it was primarily black Baptist organized and run. Yet Sujay and a couple of her bodacious girlfriends kept attending. And, on this one night, God showed up and showed out at the Hampton Conference.

A black male seminary professor, the Rev. Dr. James Forbes, now the pastor of the Riverside Church in New York City, was asked to preach at the conference. His scriptural text for the night was found in Luke 4:18–19, where the Bread of Life makes this grand announcement: "God's Spirit is on me. God has chosen me to preach the message of good news to the poor; sent me to announce pardon to prisoners and recover the sight of the blind, to set the burdened and battered free, to announce, 'This is God's year to act!" Rev. Forbes asked Sujay to come to the pulpit and to read the Holy Scriptures!

The "Big Boys" began to whisper among themselves, "What is he trying to do?" "Who is this woman who dares to mount the sacred desk?" "What's going on here?" A hush soon fell over the audience as Rev. Forbes' "teammate," Sujay, walked with dignity to the platform, read the passage, and returned to her seat. Life went on, as usual.

Sujay broke the mold that night for women clergy. And yet she wanted more than she had just experienced. She had crossed into a different dimension. She had tasted a tiny crumb of bread. Many of us, myself included, would not attend the conference. It was too rigid and too hostile. But Sujay went back year after year. She wore them down with her quiet resistance and winning smile.

Finally, her local pastor ordained her. It took New York by storm. Then they gave her a huge, almost empty church called Mariner's Temple. They felt she would go there, become disgusted, fail, and disappear. Sujay's communication background and her leadership skills and her quiet time with God led her to begin a Wednesday noon, one-hour worship service for people who worked downtown. That worship service grew into hundreds of people with a gigantic choir. The "boys" had to take notice! Girlfriend was passing out Bread!

Sujay loves to train others. She has a winning personality and attracts those who want to learn how the best do it. She was selected by Judson Press to lend her gift of leadership to compiling a work that would feed the hunger of women of color. *Sister to Sister Devotions, Vol. 1* became a best-seller!

She drew the attention of the New York police department and became their chaplain. She drew the attention of the White House and served on President Clinton's Commission on Race as the only woman of color and the only clergy. Then, she left Mariner's Temple and began a church of her own, the Bronx Christian Fellowship. She married and had two sons. She continued drawing others into her circle of leadership. She was able to lead and to delegate authority. She kept eating Bread and breaking off pieces for others.

All along her journey Sujay surrounded herself with a group of covenant community. Other clergy women who wanted more leadership opportunities became her network of visioning, dreaming, planning various strategies, goal setting, telephoning, cheerleading, and praying. Bishop Vashti McKenzie was her sister-friend before they both moved into the spotlight. Dr. Carolyn Showell, an audacious combination of Ph.D. in psychology and a grounding in the theology of the apostolic church, was praying with and for her over the years. Psalmist Sydney Evans, a praying woman, has been enlisting the hosts of heaven on her behalf when most of us didn't know her name. And Dr. Leah White, a short black Baptist pastor-teacher, has carried this battle in her heart over the years. Leadership is never a solo feat. If anyone knows this, it's successful women in the Church.

Sujay kept being faithful in her attendance to the Hampton Minister's Conference and Musician's Guild. She became the elected secretary. Then she became the elected vice-president. And in 2001, I was present as President Walter S. Thomas made the motion to accept the recommendation of the nominating committee that Rev. Dr. Suzan Johnson Cook be made the first woman to serve as president!

Just as Boaz was the "kinsman-redeemer" in the Ruth story, there must be told the story of Walter S. Thomas' commitment to "help the sistas out!" It is no accident, coincidence, or trick of fate that Sujay was set in place to become president. Walter and several other "wise men" were key in designing the multiyear strategies that allowed Sujay's name to even be put on the ballot! It is no secret that God designed men and women to work together, to live together, and to do Church together. Walter is a masterful leader and Sujay's election was one of his very deliberate goals.

I was enabled to hand President Johnson-Cook some Kleenex as all of us clergy women cried with joy at one who had broken an eighty-eight-year "males only" tradition. As a female leader she was able to shed a few tears, but the role of a female president is to be in charge and to be "a pretty woman in the pulpit"! (At least that's what I told her as she wiped her face and we continued to cry!)

The installation of President Johnson-Cook was held on opening night of the Hampton Conference in 2003. AME Bishop John Bryant presided. Mrs. Coretta Scott King, Mrs. Dorothy Height, and presidential candidate Carol Mosely Braun all brought greetings to a packed conference center that included Sujay's good friends Bishop Vashti McKenzie, the first woman elected to the episcopacy in the AME denomination, Ms. Yolanda King, and Dr. Carolyn Showell. It was, of course, a stellar night.

Pastor James Forbes introduced the woman who had read scripture for him twenty long, training years before. Then, she, with grace, dignity, and an award-winning smile, introduced us to her all-male cabinet, every one of them a fine looking and distinguished pastor. She knows the meaning of teamwork. She is well acquainted with leadership. And she is continuing to make "her story" known in the world.

Sujay preached that night about "Making the Connection: A New Attitude." She utilized scripture, of course, as she's a preaching woman. She told the story of Moses' death and Joshua being called to leadership as the one responsible to take the Jews into the promised land. She talked about how the week before she had called a friend to inform him that her fears had *almost* brought her to the point of resigning. However, she knew that God had called her to lead the conference to a new place. So she interlaced her message with the words of Pattie LaBelle's song, "I've Got a New Attitude!" She declared, before the full house, that there was no returning to the good old days of "men only!" She told the crowd that we have a new and different river to cross, and that we could stay on this side or cross over with her. She gave us all a choice. She declared that she was not going backwards, but had traveled forward all the way to Wonderful! She's ready, capable, and willing to lead!

LET'S PAUSE AND BREATHE!

1. Who or what is urging you to return to "the good old days?"
2. As you stand at the crossroad, take a serious look at what's behind you. Was it good enough to return to and start over again?
3. Can you even begin to imagine what might be ahead if you go in a different direction?
4. Have you been at this same crossroad before?
5. How did you make it back here again?
6. Who are the role models who can assist your journey through this advent to new, better, and more fulfilling?
7. Remember that if you keep doing what you've done, you will only get what you've already had. "They" say this is the sign of being an idiot! At the crossroads God wants to enlarge your territory. Look ahead. What do you see if you go in another direction?

_____

_____

_____

_____

_____

_____

_____

_____

_____

_____

_____

The reason that there are stop signs at crossroads is to give us the option of considering going in a different direction.

In the movie, *Do the Right Thing*, the contemporary, controversial director Spike Lee presents the audience with a wonderfully moving scene involving the lead character's sister. She is braiding the hair of another woman, a senior citizen, on the front steps of her home. Even though the end result is intended to be a new hairdo, the older woman shares her experienced wisdom with the younger woman, and the younger woman shares her hopes and dreams with the older woman. Dreams realized are in the presence of dreams yet to be born. It is an intergenerational exchange where wisdom and the search for it are carefully juxtaposed.

—Suzan D. Johnson-Cook, *Preaching in Two Voices*

TWO

THE SEASON OF CHRISTMAS

WONDER GIFT!

"I will not turn back"

The Chinese say that a journey of a thousand miles begins with one step. That one step towards Bethlehem and Ruth's destiny begin a season of birthing new and different ways to spread the news of Wonderful for Ruth and Naomi. Christmas is not simply one day. Christmas is a season of our celebrating the greatest gift the world has ever known. For God so loved us that Jesus, the Only Begotten Son, was given as our gift of salvation. God so blessed us with the gift of divinity wrapped in human flesh that the womb of Ruth was necessary to bring Jesus into the world. Not only was she going to be a gift to Naomi, but in the season of Christmas God had a wonderful gift waiting for her!

Isn't it amazing how life can change so swiftly for us? One day, Ruth was home in Moab. The next day, her "life script" had been torn to pieces. She didn't know her role any longer, but she knew that she was willing to take a lead role in the lives of both herself and Naomi. What if she had decided to turn around and go backwards? Where would the story of Jesus have had to detour if Ruth had not wanted to go on the adventure of Christmas?

My sista Rev. Louisa Martin, who has a daily e-devotional called "A Byte to Chew," sent one quote that continues to ring in my spirit. It talked about how we have to be willing to give up the life we have already planned if we want to be led by God into our destiny! This was mind-blowing in its simplicity. For we call things into being with our thoughts and our words. We are just that powerful, for we are like God! So, if I want to go to Wonderful (and I do!), it means relinquishing my dream for the dream God has for me!

We never know how life will move us along. We may plan and have goals and even hold winning strategies. But life is not fair. Life has its own set of rules. Like Ruth, often we find our options limited and our choices few. Go back? Go forward? Stand still? There were not a lot of other choices before Ruth. With a bad situation behind her and an unknown one before her, the girl did not have a lot of wiggle room! Our only assurance comes from knowing that when we are down to almost nothing, God is up to something bigger than we can ever imagine.

My certainty is that God is always about increase! God does not send us into periods of decrease without reason and blessings in our learned lessons! Oft times our poor stewardship or our robbing God of tithes and offerings might force us into periods of decrease. However, God is always about adding. The only thing God wants to take away is our sin! Ruth was not a "homegrown" Jewish woman. She had watched and listened to the conversations from her spouse and his family. It is certain that she worshipped when they worshipped. But it could have been a "let's pretend" worship. For Naomi told them to return to their families and their gods. Ruth decided to take a chance on the birthing God. Ruth threw in her lot with the One who created life in the first place. With her determination to move into a new and strange culture, Ruth gave birth to a new self.

Whoopi Goldberg starred in the movie *Ghosts of Mississippi*, which is now on video. It is the true and moving story of the cold-blooded murder of a Mississippi freedom fighter, Megar Lee Evers. It is the true and moving story of a thirty-year battle to convict his murderer, one Mr. Delacrow. This personal fight has been waged by Mrs. Merlie Evans, a wife, mother, educator, and civil rights warrior. Her love for her husband, her family, and her people compelled her to continue seeking the conviction of the man who bragged about " killing a nigger."

After Mr. Delacrow was tried and set free by a jury of his peers on two occasions, the new lawyer of Mrs. Evers approached Mr. Delacrow in the men's toilet and asked him how he could kill one of God's wonderful creatures in cold blood, like he was a deer? Mr. Delacrow turned and began to talk about the awesome God who formed a beautiful creature like a deer. Mr. Delacrow said that he had too much respect for God and for God's creation to ever shoot down a deer. "But," he said, "shooting a nigger was another matter."

WE ARE GOD'S GIFTS TO EACH OTHER

Isn't it amazing that we can recognize God in the creatures of nature and yet miss the wonders of God in both ourselves and in relationships with other human beings? It's a wonder that God continues to allow the beauty of the world to stand in its entire splendor as we continue to deny the common bond and the common blood that unites us. Ruth had appropriated the quoted words of the psalmist, who writes in Psalm 139 that we are each fearfully and wonderfully made! The "fearfully made" phrase means that we are to be awestruck about all of God's work. The word "wonderfully" can also be translated as "beautifully"! Ruth saw the beauty in Naomi. For Ruth recognized that she was wonderfully made herself!

Psalm 139 says that each one of God's people is special, unique, and a miracle of Love Divine. What happens to us too often is that we fail to realize who we are and whose we are. Our hearts can become filled with envy of others until we cannot see or realize our own unique qualities. Our hearts can become so closed to the love that can flow our way from others that we fail to understand that when we shut out relationships with those who are different from us, we also shut out God!

God's *imago dei*, or divine image, is stamped within each one of us born into the world. A piece of God, called the "wonderful spark," is in every human being. We each have the ability to illuminate God's presence within the world community. It only requires our being open, like Ruth, to various relationships that allow us to see God in others. It mandates that we are willing to stretch in order to hear God in the native tongues of others. It requires being able to touch God as we reach out and develop loving, caring human relationships, both within our own racial, cultural, ethnic group and within the wider world community. For it was only God who was able to create the universe without the aid of images, memory, or prior experiences! All the rest of us need to use our imagination!

Cheryl Forbes, speaking theologically, says:

> Imagination is the imago dei in us. It marks us as God's human creatures. It helps us know God, to receive God's grace, to worship God, and to see life through the eyes of God. That means, imagination is a way of seeing life—or ways of seeing life. . . . Imagination is our means of grace and our hope of glory. It humanizes us in the truest meaning of that word—by making us more like Christ, the only completely imaginative person who ever lived. . . . What imagination helps us see is that any life, no matter how ordinary, is extraordinary with God, who shattered ordinariness with the Incarnation. . . . Our Christian faith and life is a mystery. . . . The first and strongest image is that of the Last Supper or the Eucharist.
>
> We reenact the Lord's final Passover with his disciples when we celebrate Communion. The Jews, of course, were reenacting part of their ancient history. Our meal, the Lord's Supper, uses the basic elements of life—bread and wine, food and drink. These are the images of Christ's body and blood.[1]

The wonder in our journey with Ruth is that without having a full sense of what the Passover would mean to her life, she was willing, able, and capable of imagining that a new place, a new time, and a new situation would provide for both she and Naomi the basic elements of their lives, bread and wine, food and drink. She saw images of what could be before she ever left the crossroads.

Forbes goes on to tell readers that without the "why not" and the "I wonder what would happen if" questions there would be few if any new discoveries. For every new venture is fueled by curiosity, new ideas, and a simple appreciation for life coupled with an educated understanding of its simplicity. These qualities "mark nearly every example of a person who lives imaginatively. Imagination is God's common grace at work."[2]

"Imagination never sleeps. . . . Imagination is a state of being, a habit of the mind. . . . Imagination works two ways, helping us see an idea whole . . . and helping us to recognize that something can be made of a mistake," prompts Forbes, who uses an illustration from Lewis Carroll's work *Through The Looking Glass*.[3]

The Queen is speaking to Alice: "'I can't believe that' said Alice. 'Can't you?' the Queen said in a pitying tone. 'Try again: draw a long breath and shut your eyes.' Alice laughed. 'There's no use trying,' she said; 'One can't believe impossible things.' 'I daresay you haven't much practice,' said the Queen. 'When I was your age, I always did it for half-an-hour a day. Why sometimes I've believed as many as six impossible things before breakfast.'"[4] Ruth had the Queen's capacity for believing in what Naomi thought was impossible!

Orpah, for whatever reason, did not recognize her own capacity of "wonderfulness." She turned back and left Naomi to fend for herself. Ruth, on the other hand, was capable of knowing, saying, and claiming the divine spark, the *imago dei,* within herself so that she had appreciation for the wonder that had led her mother-in-law to stand on the brink of despair, desolation, and depression.

As Ruth looked at the woman who had lost everything and everyone close to her, she saw the pain. She was able to reach from that deep *imago dei* place within herself to offer a piece of her untapped wonder to Naomi. Christmas had come. She was Naomi's gift. As in the song, "Lean On Me," Ruth offered a strong and powerful hand to Naomi as they made the journey to Wonderful.

A CONTEMPORARY RUTH

Daisybelle is her name. She was born into a huge family in a small, rural town in Alabama. There was a mother and a father who farmed. The father was also a local pastor who preached at area churches. But, with so many mouths to feed, there was seldom enough to eat, and there was always work to be done. They nicknamed Daisybelle "Red," for she was a light-skinned African American, stocky and filled with anger at the whole wide world.

Daisybelle was in the middle of this huge family. There were older siblings, but she became the "mother" of those under her. She was feisty and an able fighter. She didn't cotton to foolishness and had a quick mouth and quicker fist. She stayed in trouble at school, and she was never far from trouble at home. There seemed to be a perpetual famine in their home. A famine of food. A famine of time for her. A famine of affection. A famine of self-esteem. A famine of accepting love that fostered positive self-confidence.

Many days the school was not a safe environment for Daisybelle. She would be sent to the school principal and made to sit in the office. It was there that she begin to find pieces of nourishing bread. The principal began to make room in her heart for this little lost girl. She began to allow her to come to her home on weekends to help with chores. Then Daisybelle was able to begin saving money. She began to see how others lived where there was no famine. And the principal begin to whisper words of encouragement to Daisybelle in their time alone.

"Daisybelle, you have 'famousity' in you. I see it." These words began to stick with the girl and to ring in her ears. When away from the principal's sight, out of the principal's view, and far from her visible influence, the words continued to flow and to flourish, calling forth leadership abilities from within Daisybelle that others could not see. One day, while walking in her dad's footsteps in the freshly plowed fields at home, Daisybelle made a decision to go and find the land of bread. "I'll never be hungry again. I'm not living in a state of famine all my life."

Daisybelle dropped out of high school in her junior year to go and become a nanny in New York City. A cousin had been working in a home there for some years and decided to get married. She called and asked if Daisybelle would like a job. Daisybelle remembered her covenant to seek new bread. She decided to go to New York. She was on her way to Wonderful!

No Greyhound bus came to the little town of her birth. A neighbor had to drive Daisybelle and her mother to the next town to catch the bus. Daisybelle had saved her money from the principal, bought herself a few clothes, and paid for her own ticket. When the bus arrived, she kissed her mother good-bye and climbed upon the bus. She sat in the first seat, across from the driver. Her mother began to wave, saying, "Move back. Move back."

It didn't cross Daisybelle's mind that segregation laws forbade her riding in the front of a bus in Alabama. She had never been on a bus trip before and she wanted to see all the sights and ask the driver questions. Others kept getting on the bus as she tried to ignore her mother's constant waving.

Then Daisybelle noticed the tears on her mother's face and the look of fright. This was more than a "My child is leaving me" look in her eyes! Daisybelle finally got the message and noticed that there were no other people who looked like her in the front of the bus. She took her luggage and moved to a more appropriate seat. Her mother's look changed to relief as the bus to "bread" took off down the road.

When she got to New York City, a letter from her cousin instructed her to take a train and then to catch a cab. She had never done either. But she insists that God put the right train conductor and the right cab driver in place just for her. She made it to her destination, the home of a Mafia leader and his family! Daisybelle landed in the house of much bread and lived there for a year.

She learned how to set a proper table and to prepare a good meal. She learned how to dress the children in decent apparel. She learned how to shop at the "good" stores. She ordered groceries and learned to give instructions. She was well groomed and attended worship services in the big city and watched an entirely different black culture. After a year, she went home to finish school.

Daisybelle got a scholarship to Tuskeegee Institute. She got a Master's degree in psychology. Then she went to work and taught elementary school for twenty-two years. She married for the first time at forty-plus. She moved to a foreign land and went to seminary. She was ordained. She began an area-wide ministry to women, along with the Voices of Triumph Drama Company.

Today Daisybelle puts on dinner theater performances that are more than fabulous. She and her spouse, Nelson, travel the country as she portrays the history of Sojourner Truth, Mary McCleod Bethune, and Fannie Lou Hamer at college campuses and other institutions of higher learning.

Last year, this no longer country "young woman," returned home to Alabama. As her mother is aging, Daisybelle and Nelson decided to leave the familiarity of the north and return to the place of her first roots, where "famousity" was first spoken into her ears, invested into her life, and woven into her spirit. Girlfriend refused to leave her mother alone. She went away from home, in order to return home more qualified to be of assistance, not to just her mom, but to the entire community of Wonderful, everywhere!

LET'S PAUSE AND BREATHE!

1. Ruth had to separate from Orpah, her parents, and her gods in order to move forward. What are you being called to leave behind as you journey to Wonderful?

2. In the season of Christmas we exchange gifts. If you were gift-wrapped and presented to Jesus this day, what would you look like?

3. In the season of Christmas we know that Jesus is born anew. How have you birthed the Living Christ in the last week?

4. Angels play a huge role in the Christmas story. What "angelic" visitors have come your way with messages of good news within the past week?

5. Music is important to the birth narrative. What is the song that you are humming and singing even when you are not consciously aware of it?

6. Ruth made a declaration not to turn back and leave Naomi. It was a strong promise. Who have you broken a promise to in the past week? We are hard on those who break promises to us. Now, what will you do to make amends?

7. What "wonderful" person have you missed recently because he or she was a bit too different for you? Could that have been God that you missed?

8. Most of us get to the crossroads and see the large red stop sign. However, most of us continue going in the direction that will carry us to "same and familiar." Ruth said she would go in a different direction. Where will a new direction carry you? What are some of the pregnant possibilities being born from within you?

Wonderful requires a companion. Wonderful demands someone who can lead sometimes. Wonderful are good friends who love us with all of our faults and failures. Who are some possible companions? Remember to look for those who will offer comfort, confrontation, collaboration, clarity, and celebration. It's difficult to find all these characteristics in one person. Choose carefully and wisely. From both your personal (family and friends) and professional (include Church and work affiliations) associations, name two people in each category:

Two comforting friends:

Two confronting friends:

Two collaborating friends:

Two clarifying friends:

Two celebrating friends:

We all stand on the shoulders of our ancestors as we support future generations. Knowing where we come from helps to determine where we are going. We all belong somewhere and to someone: interconnections help establish our roots. We did not come along alone; we are joined to each other by the lines of life.

— Byllye Avery, *An Altar of Words*

THREE

THE SEASON OF EPIPHANY

WONDER IS A STATE OF MIND

"Where you go, I will go"

R uth had never been out of Moab. She had been born in Moab. She had been raised in Moab. It is pretty clear that she had meant to marry, have a family, and die in Moab. But Life called. Ruth answered.

What most of us don't know is that Moab was a place renowned for its sensual, sexually immoral habits, culture, and mores. Moab was not known for being a "nice" place. The Jews, with a high sense of moral values, had a decree that other Gentiles could be converted to Judaism within two generations. However, the news about Moab was so distasteful that it required ten generations for a Moabite to convert!

When Ruth left Moab she was well aware that she would not be easily integrated into the place that judged "her kind" so harshly. Yet, she had a made up her mind to see this journey through! The power of the story of God had grabbed her and pulled her into the mystery of the Most High God!

Wonder is a state of mind that requires the use of our imagination. We are taught that day dreaming is not quite proper. We are told to stay focused. We are told to act like adults. But the truth is that if we want to travel further than the limits of our parents' lives we have to use our imagination and pretend to be different. If we have any thoughts of moving beyond the boundaries of where we were born and how we were raised, we have to use the magic of our imagination.

Epiphany is the story of the Wise who came following a star to discover a King. They came because they had heard the story. Story has the power to transport us. Story has the ability to take us to a different place. Story has the capacity to provide a variety of new beginnings and to even change poor endings. Ruth had been captured by Naomi's story of God in Bethlehem. Her imagination took her to Bethlehem. She longed to be included in history.

Introducing her work *If It Wasn't for the Woman,* minister and sociology professor Dr. Cheryl Townsend Gilkes provides us with her insight regarding women of color and the power of the God story throughout the history of the American black Church.

> The overwhelming majority of black women who have contributed to building their communities and moving their children and others forward have not left written records of their activism. Yet, they are not invisible. They publicly present themselves on the various occasions of public ritual such as Women's Day and awards ceremonies when they can be visible to and appreciated by the beneficiaries of their labors. When their power and effectiveness become too visible for others to bear to acknowledge because, as one male board member told the female founder and director of the agency on whose board she had placed him, 'it looks bad for the race.' These women will remind us in a variety of ways that if it wasn't for the women . . . there would be no church!
>
> In every aspect of African American life and history black women have been a significant force, the something within. In every organization where they are present, they have been the key actors responsible for the integrity and efficacy of the operations. According to civil rights folk-

lore, one famous leader said that if the women ever left the movement, he was going with them, because nothing was going to happen without the women. Black women have been either invisible to researchers who have approached the history and social life of black people armed with presumptions of mainstream social science, or these women's visibility has been overlooked as unimportant to the larger questions governing the research. . . . Yet in every national convocation . . . narratives of women's enterprise and activism that had strengthened, shaped, transformed, and sustained the organization were embedded in their histories.[1]

Lucy E. Campbell, way back in the day, wrote a song that contains Cheryl's primary thought about the role of women in the Church:

Something within me that holdeth the reins.
Something within me that banishes pain.
Something within me that I cannot explain.
All that I know there is something within.[2]

CAN YOU IMAGINE A NEW DAY?

As the group of weary women stood at the crossroads, one of them could not imagine a new future. Her mind was closed to the story of "there." She was stuck in the "here and now." As bad as the present seemed to Orpah, she was familiar with it. She knew the lay of the land. She was well acquainted with the landscape and the terrain. Therefore, she was captured by her lack of imagination. For us, she will always be a symbol of "what if" or "if only." Try to imagine the best ending for her story. It will require a great sense of wonder to make it one that was "happy ever after!"

On the other hand there was Ruth, who had paid close attention to the ways in which her spouse and his family had talked of Bethlehem, the land of bread. They had woven their story into the very fabric of her life. She had lifted strands from each of them and allowed them to pull her into the mystery of another way, another life, and another God. When Naomi tried to prevent her from following the new story line, she quickly responded, "I won't turn back! Where you go, I will go!"

Ruth had to have speculated ways that she could become part of a new beginning. For the old Ruth was going to be left behind. There was nothing of Moab that she would carry, with the exception of memories and a few wrapped trinkets. But she "saw" herself being able to support both Naomi and herself. She "saw" that she could provide the means for their welfare. She "saw" that she had enough stamina to be sufficient for their new way of life. Her imagination had to have been working overtime. And she was carried forward by a sense of wonder.

A WONDER-FILLED SEASON

Epiphany is a wonder-filled season. It is that time of the Christian year when different facets of Jesus are shown through the scriptures. For the known world came to see this new King. The Wise ventured from long distances. The Wise traveled for years, following a star. The Wise were not Jews, but Gentiles. As a matter of fact they were star gazers, more closely associated to astrology than to religious matters. But they came because they had heard the King's story! They imaged their journey individually and then got together and made the trip successfully.

In the Greco-Roman world, this time of year was when political dignitaries made their annual visit. The people imagined better conditions. The people imagined favor and salvation from oppression. The people imagined good will toward them during this period. So Epiphany is a time when twinkling stars yet shine. Epiphany is the season when God expects us to be the shining stars! Epiphany is the season when God imagines that the world will become better due to our loving acts. And Epiphany is the season when God imagines that we will show favor and justice in the world. The Wise yet seek to follow their star to an unknown destiny.

"I wonder where we will live." "I wonder where I will be able to find work." "I wonder how I will be judged in a foreign land." "I wonder if I will be accepted." "I wonder . . ." The list of wonder is long, almost inexhaustible. But the sense of varied possibilities is also almost inexhaustible.

TWINKLE, TWINKLE BRIGHT STAR

Without a clear crisis, brought about by Naomi's decision and depression, Ruth would never have discovered who she was and what she was capable of handling. When the sun shines in the heat of the day, no one can see the twinkling of the stars. Some things are only able to be seen when the lights go out and the darkness is everywhere. The moon and the stars only come out at night. The whippoorwill only sings at night. The owl hoots its warning call in the night. Night crawlers dare to roam only under the cloud of darkness. And our best is only called forth when it's night within our soul! When the night comes, and the lights go out, we are forced to shine from within. Ruth began to twinkle when Naomi declared, "It's nighttime in my spirit."

Where Naomi's storyline ends, Ruth's begins. It seems that we journey together in order to be bound in covenant relationship. "One cannot break a threefold cord. " (Ecc. 4:12, *The Message*). This is the power of community. This is the essential point of our walking together toward our destiny. For my destiny is intertwined with yours. Your destiny is intertwined with mine. There are no superstars on the journey to Wonderful! There are only those individuals who pay attention and pull alongside of one who wants to drop out of line.

We were in Haiti on a mission trip and went to take supplies as we visited a mountain elementary school. The van took us as far up the mountain as it was able until the narrow road became impossible. We walked the next five miles straight up. I thought it would be a breeze to walk back to the van. But the elevation worked on our breathing. For those of us who were not veteran walkers the thin air begin to take its toll.

I felt like stopping. I didn't feel that I could make it. Chuck was having trouble too. But there was a younger brother, Abiade, who was a practiced runner. Abiade took off his shirt and told me to put my hand on his shoulder and he pulled me along until I could catch my breath. When we stopped for a spell, he would run ahead to check the path and come back and say, "We're almost there." (He lied a lot!) Then he pulled me further down the mountainside. We made it back to the van together. (I promised myself that I would not visit any more mountain schools!) Seeing the van and sitting in the van was "Wonderful"!

The essential element of the story is that having a shoulder to lean upon is the basis of community. We all get tired and change our names to "Bitter." We all have episodes of depression, gloom, weariness, and despair. We are human. This is part of the human experience. Even Jesus got weary, disgusted, and angry. Yet he kept a community close around him. He checked in with them and took them along on his three-year journey. The Bible recalls that on the night of his betrayal, he asked his disciples to accompany him to the Garden as he prayed. He needed their shoulders to lean upon!

That Jesus needed them did not dawn upon them until much later in the story. But Ruth discovered Naomi's need for her at the crossroads. "I will not let you down." This was her commitment. "I will not leave you alone. Where you go, I will go too!" This was her promise. "I won't allow you to try and make this journey on your own. I'm going with you all the way. Your story is my story from here on out." This was a covenant relationship. They didn't know it, they had no clue that day of the new story they were creating. But these two women, sisters now, were on their way to Wonderful!

A CONTEMPORARY RUTH: WHO WILL HELP MS. CHICKEN?

Once upon a time there was a barnyard and it was filled with all sorts of little creatures. There were short ones and tall ones. There were little ones and there were large ones. There were industrious ones and there were lazy ones. There were the ones who got along with everyone and of course there were the ones who got along with none of the others. There were nice ones and there were nasty ones. There were ones who loved belonging to this particular barnyard and there were those who were forever looking for the next sale. The barnyard was sort of like the church, for they were all God's creatures, despite their outlook on life.

The barnyard was a safe place for many years. The animals were well kept, well groomed, and well fed. But, like every place else, the economy took a dip. The animals' troughs began to be empty more than filled. The days seemed to grow longer and the animals became both hungry and angry. They began to question who was responsible for their empty troughs. They began to find fault, to point fingers, and to make up reasons that they were not being fed. One chicken began to say, "There is plenty of land. Who will help me go and find grain?" Well, nobody volunteered. The chicken said it again, for she was sure that they had not understood her statement. "There is plenty of land. Who will help me go and find grain?" The silence was very loud.

Off went the little chicken in search for grain. And, of course, if you seek, you will find. Ms. Chicken found some grain. She went back to the barnyard and began to prepare a plot of ground for planting. None of the other animals came to help her. She plowed alone. She planted alone. She watered alone. She pulled weeds alone. She gathered in the wheat alone. She took the wheat to the mill and ground it alone. She took the ground flour home and made some hot, buttered sweet rolls and baked them in the oven alone. Then the scent of the baking bread got plenty of attention from hungry and lazy barnyard animals.

Soon there was a knock at Ms. Chicken's door and when she opened it there stood all the other animals. The one selected to be spokesperson stepped right up and began to talk about "community values." They all made a case for the Christian ethic of sharing. And of course they played on the fact that they were very hungry and were her neighbors. She stood and listened to all the good reasons. She never interrupted one time. When the spokesperson finished, Ms. Chicken said very quietly, "To the laborer belongs the spoils of the harvest."

Of course the animals began to shout, "What do you mean? What are you talking about?" So Ms. Chicken said, "Let me remind you that I asked all of you to take part in the search for grain and in preparing the ground. None of you wanted to help. I asked twice to make sure that you heard me. Not one of you responded. Well, I went and found the grain, alone. I came back and plowed the land, alone. I planted the grain, alone. I watered the grain daily, alone. I pulled the weeds to separate the wheat from the tare, alone. I gathered in the wheat, alone. I took the wheat to the mill and ground it all alone. I mixed the ingredients for my bread and made it alone. And, now, I will eat the fruit of my harvest all alone! You had every chance to help me and you refused!" And, with that, Sista Girl went into her house, closed her door, and ate her meal, all alone.

This is a little fairy tale taught to first and second graders about the need to offer help to others. It teaches little children that there is something called teamwork, sharing, and community. It lifts up the value of working together that makes life easier for everyone involved. This story makes us laugh. Yet, the underlying truth is not really funny. For in the Church of the Living God, makes no difference about the denomination, ethnic group, or gender; there are always those who want to share in the end product, called the harvest. Yet, there are actually very few folks who want to help get involved in the actual labor that produces the harvest.

Scripture says that Ms. Chicken is very correct in her actions, for "If you don't work, you don't eat" (2 Thess. 3:10).

It's that simple. It required much work for Ms. Chicken to get that loaf of bread. We are not talking about taking money or food stamps to buy a loaf of baked bread. That Lil Sister had to do it the old fashioned way. She had to do it from scratch. She did it the labor intensive way, with sweat equity. Girlfriend got no breaks. She had to hustle, sacrifice, and work hard. And it was not a one-time deal. She had to work diligently, every day. She produced the harvest with the help of God. For God made the grain. God made the earth. God made the rain. God gave her strength to search, find, plow, dig, plant, weed, gather, and mill. She and God were colaborers. She did her part faithfully and she reaped the harvest.

I want that hundredfold harvest, don't you? As a matter of fact, if you look at Deuteronomy 1:11, Moses prays for the people of God and says, "May the Lord, the God of your ancestors, increase you a thousand times more and bless you as . . . promised." All we have to do is help with the work of Jesus Christ.

We are not called to do it all. We are not called to do it alone. But, we are called to community and gifted by the Holy Spirit to work together to make every church a soul saving station. We all have to do our part. Jesus paid the full price for the land on Calvary. He sent the Holy Spirit to assist us in the plowing, planting, weeding, and ingathering. We all have a part to play. We cannot stand around looking, like those barnyard animals. For the summer is past. The fruit, vegetables, and grain fields are ready for harvest. The laborers are few. The question is: Who will go and help little Ms. Chicken?

LET'S PAUSE AND BREATHE

1. Twinkle, twinkle little star, God already knows who you are! What are some of the "twinkling" visions that you have smothered and allow to lie dormant?

2. Epiphany means to "see" and to "be" a shining star! When was the last time that you allowed the "flashing" part of your personality to be exposed in your circle of influence?

3. There are several women in your community who are outstanding. Name three that have been role models as "twinkling stars" for you?

4. What sets them apart? What attributes of theirs do you have within? What character traits of theirs do you exhibit? The ancestors used to give their "determinations" for the year. This was their "I will do" statements to follow through on for Jesus Christ. Name your "I will do" list for this year. These are life goals that you want to carry out.

5. Now, what small steps do you need to take in the next six months to help you reach your goal? Set monthly achievements that are required of you.

6. Using your very best "outside of the box" thinking, what would you do in the next year if all the right conditions were lined up and guaranteed for you?

Nothing in life is guaranteed but death! However, if Ruth had not made a visual image of what could be a different ending, her future would not be recorded for our benefit. Death is not the worse thing that can happen to us. The worse thing that can happen is for death to come for us and we have never really begun to live!

What a strange thing is memory, and hope; one looks backward, the other forward. The one is of today, the other is of tomorrow. Memory is history recorded in our brain, memory is a painter, it paints pictures of the past and of the day.

—Grandma Moses

FOUR

ASH WEDNESDAY

WONDERMENT!

"Where you stay, I will stay"

There are two recent publications on the market. Both of them have been released by Princeton University Press. Both of these works attempt to address the economic plight of America. Both of them seek to deal honestly, forthrightly, and candidly with a pressing social issue in our country. Both of these studies draw our attention to that dreaded "W" word, *welfare*.

Welfare—the need to take the hard-earned resources of the nation and care for a group of lazy no-accounts who just need to pull themselves up by their own bootstraps.

Welfare—that system of support provided to families and children who are needy, poverty stricken, and draining the pockets of middle Americans.

Welfare—that continuing systemic evil that has shackled millions in generational cycles of dependency upon others for their basic needs and survival.

The author of *Work and Welfare*, Robert Solow, a Nobel prize-winning economist, directs his attention to how we can get people off welfare and into self-sustaining jobs.[1] Let's not talk about the reality that most of the "new" jobs pay minimum wage, don't provide medical benefits, or don't allow folks to earn enough money to maintain their own apartments and surely not to participate in home ownership. Let's not address the reality that downsizing, economic retrenchment, and the rethinking of industrial giants have now done their part in increasing welfare rolls with formerly well-employed, independent individuals.

Let's not deal with the truth that 90 percent of the wealth in the world is in the hands of about 3 percent of the people. And most of this wealth can be directly traced back to their foreparents who exploited, stole, and enslaved less fortunate folks in order to buy the boots and the shoe laces by which they "pulled themselves up." But Mr. Solow organized his research of this cogent argument into a lecture. And he has found a ready audience to buy his book.

The other book, *It Takes a Nation*, is subtitled *A New Agenda for Fighting Poverty*. It's written from the research of Rebecca Blank.[2] This is another look at how "the haves" can reduce the number of "have nots" who require our hard-earned tax dollars and sheltered monetary gains. If I had the time, I'd really like to deal with the psychological significance behind the last names of both of these good folks, Solow and Blank. But that's an entirely different issue to address.

However, the "W" word, *welfare*, is the controversy that has even reared its ugly head in the Church. Only we don't use the "W" word. We call it tithing or giving 10 percent of our livelihood in offerings and benevolent givings. A portion of our money has to go to help others. A portion of our hard-earned dollars has to go to assist those with less. A portion of our funds, which could better be used, right here, at home, has to be sent off overseas, divided among various home mission projects, distributed to racial ethnic congregations who look nothing like us! Our money is even donated to those so-called ecumenical activities that have nothing to do with our individual denomination!

We hear the questions. "What's up with this? Why must our local congregations provide *welfare* for others who have the same opportunity to pull themselves up if they would simply get off their trifling backsides and put forth the same efforts that we do?"

Now, of course, we'd never say these sorts of harsh words out loud! We're too nice. We're too pious. We're too religious. We just decide to write smaller checks for those special appeals. Or we'll toss in a couple of dollar bills to assuage our conscience and declare that we've done our socially required part. But the reality is that apportioned giving, tithing, and special offerings are honestly forms of the "W" word. For it is *our responsibility* to share from our resources with the poor, who Christ declared would always be with us. Like the woman in Holy Scriptures who kept going before the unjust judge (Like 18:1–8), the poor keep crying out to God for relief, justice, and divine intervention. And God keeps answering their prayers through *you, me, and our apportioned giving of tithes and offering.* Friends, there is no other way!

Jesus taught the disciples, the first Church, about the power of prayer. For in the Church of the Living God there are arrogant, pious, self-righteous folks who feel that they are alright, have all the answers, and know exactly how to be in charge! They really do feel that they are morally superior to all others. "Lord, I thank you that I'm not like others in this church." He talks to them about the unjust judge who had no regard for God nor people. Then, he moves to the heart of the issue. The scripture says, "Jesus told this parable to some who trusted in themselves that they were righteous and regarded others with contempt" (Luke 18:9).

We don't expect Jesus to deal with us in a harsh and direct manner. We want to hear a nice Jesus. We want an affirming Jesus. We want a Jesus who will talk about our blessings and our prosperity. But Jesus is always honest. Jesus is always real. Jesus is authentic about our shortcomings. So Jesus comes to deal with our self-righteous pride. He comes to remind each one of us that *we* are on the "W" word, *welfare.*

The breath we breathe is from the *public welfare* of our God.

The energy that sustains our productivity and intelligence is directly from the *public welfare* of our God.

The food we eat, the harvest we reap, the earth, its seeds and grains that reproduce—it all comes from the *public welfare* of our God.

The clothes we wear, the houses we live in, the cars we drive, the church buildings we inhabit, the money we make, the jobs we hold—all come to us by way of God's *public welfare*.

Jesus says don't get so arrogant that you forget that you exist off the "W" word of a generous and loving God.

Jesus also says don't get so stuck on stupid till you fall into the pitiful state of the Pharisee. He tells in Luke 18:10–14 about the Pharisee, a Temple leader, a solid church member, who stood in the church and prayed, "God, I thank you that I'm not welfare dependent. I thank you, God, that I have arrived. I thank you, God, that I've pulled myself up by my own bootstraps. I thank you, God, that my strength is my own; my resources are my own and my intelligence is my own. I'm not like those who need you. Truly, I thank you that I'm not a thief, a rogue, and adulterer. I am a good church member. Check out my attendance record. You can even look at my fiscal records. I don't just pledge, I pay tithes. Check me out, God, I'm much better than this person standing there who is seeking welfare from you!"

On the other hand, there stood the bonafide thief. He was a certified needy person. And he was a self-identified welfare seeker. He prayed, "God, be merciful to me, a sinner. God, be mindful of me, a needy individual. God, take notice of me, one who is dependent upon your welfare."

And, shock of shocks: Jesus says, "I tell you, the one who is welfare dependent went home with an answered prayer! The other went home, but know that God's got something in store for him. For all who feel that they don't need God's welfare will be brought down. But all those who understand, affirm, and claim that all that they have comes from God will be lifted up, carried on eagles wings, and made to shine like the sun."

The welfare program of God works. The welfare program of God continues. The welfare program of God has an established cycle:

1. God gives to us.
2. We work with what we get.
3. We share what we have with others.

As we give, God gives to us. It's called the law of sowing and reaping. It's called apportioned living. It's apportioned giving. It's the big time, all the time "W" word.

WE NEED WELFARE

My sisters, if we're too good to cooperate with God's welfare plan, then we are Pharisees and Jesus has full contempt for us! Today, the invitation is to recognize just how dependent we are upon God. We need to recognize that our salvation has come into the world only because of God's welfare. For while we were yet sinners, God loved us so much . . . until the master welfare plan was put into effect. God gave us Jesus, the Only Begotten Son. And Jesus gave his whole life as a ransom for you and me.

There is no question. There is no debate. There is no compromise position. Giving to others is the very least that we can do. Apportioned living by volunteering and apportioned giving through tithing and offerings is our legacy. This is why it is recorded that Ruth told Naomi, "where you stay, I will stay." In today's language she would say, "Whoever provides welfare for you in Bethlehem, I will abide by the rules of their home also."

What Ruth understood was that in being a leader she had to first of all establish a foothold in a new place. So many of us receive promotions, new opportunities, and new positions and the very first thing we tend to do is hurry to change things to suit us! Ruth teaches us that this is not a smart move. When we enter into new situations, places, and circumstances, we need to learn how to "be still, and see the salvation of God" (Psalm 46:10, *The Message*).

God was in Bethlehem when Naomi had left many years prior. Ruth determined that God was yet operating, without her assistance, in Bethlehem. She was willing to go into Bethlehem and have a "look see." A "look see" is a time of ascertaining the culture of the new place. Something was happening before we arrived on the scene! A "look see" permits us to get acquainted with our team members and to allow them to realize our respect for them, their wisdom, and their history in the place where we are the newcomers. A "look see" helps us to take careful notes of what is important to those already established in that place and to seek their input as to how change can best be made.

Have you ever noticed that God permits us a "look see" even as the weather in our area begins to change? We seldom find God giving us sudden change without warning. But the changing air, the look of the leaves, and the shifting of the winds whisper, "Get ready for change!" In the same way, when we come on the scene, especially in a diversity situation, everyone is already aware that "change" has occurred. It is a primary principle that we move slowly and take a "look see," knowing that those already established folks are taking a "look see" at us!

To receive and to give hospitality has been a benchmark of the Jews. For we recall that they were wilderness wanderers for over forty years and provided hospitality by the Almighty. They had been instructed to be welcoming to the foreigner and the sojourners in their midst. All throughout the history of their chronicles, they are reminded over and over to be hospitable and charitable to all.

Elimelech owned land in Bethlehem, but we must use our imagination to see what uncared-for, neglected, and dilapidated property would have become in ten years of absence. There was no way that these two women would be allowed to stay in a place that had been unkempt for such a long period of time. It was certain that when they reached the land of Naomi's home, they would be entitled to the welfare of some kind soul.

We have no record of their conversation on the journey. We are not given details of how many days it took for them to make this trip. We have no public announcement of who opened their home and took them in when they arrived. But we know that a welcome mat was put out. And we know that wherever Naomi stayed, Ruth put herself into subjection to the rules of this home.

This meant that she had to learn the way of the woman of the house. This meant that she had little room for doing things her way or even the way that Naomi had shown her in Moab. This meant that she placed herself under the supervision of Naomi and whoever the wife was who took them in and made them welcome. Where she was told to sleep, she slept. Whatever duties were assigned her, she did. What she was given to eat, she ate with gratitude. For she was on welfare. Naomi was too! They were in Wonderful Bethlehem. But they were living with restrictions, and they were not in their own home.

HUMAN LIMITATIONS

Ash Wednesday comes to remind us that we don't own the tent in which our spirit is housed. Ash Wednesday comes to help us understand that our flesh is only on loan to us. Ash Wednesday comes to assist us in comprehending that we are strangers in a hostile land and that heaven is our soul's home. Ash Wednesday has us marked with ashes so that we will remember that God has promised to never leave us or to forsake us and that as long as we are in this body, God is with us. This is welfare at its best!

We can lean and depend upon God being gracious to us. We can trust that God has the best in mind for us. We can see God's faithfulness to us in the days gone by. And we can acknowledge God in all our ways and the Holy Spirit will guide us day by day. This is the most gracious hospitality of God, shown to us on a daily basis.

In Ruth's trust of Naomi's relationships in Bethlehem, she opened herself to receive God's welfare plan and generous hospitality towards her. She found that God's welfare system is more than wonderful!

A CONTEMPORARY RUTH

My friend's name was Constance Wilkerson. We walked the journey of ministry as women for many years together. Connie was one of those women that I could be very honest with and have her accept me anyway. It was because of her challenge to me that this very book was written! Connie called me to face the parts of me that had died and those that yet had to die! Connie was one of my sisters who did not mind facing the changing seasons of our life with gusto and with flair.

Connie was a teaching preacher. She did not play with God's Word. It was her meat day and night. At my last installation worship, she was there to lay hands on me and to pray for Mista

Chuck and me. She introduced me to her friend, Lynn Luelen, who has become my friend. Connie was a connecting link among many of us. I was so proud of her when God called her and she answered that call to begin to pastor a congregation, Gate of Heaven, in Flint, Michigan.

Let me give you some background. Lynn had been Connie's friend for almost thirty years. For many years they had been church members at New Jerusalem Baptist Church in Flint, working in Christian Education ministries as a team. Connie had been ordained and felt the urge to begin her own congregation. Lynn went to minister with her as a servant, a helper, the coordinator of praise and worship tape ministry. She didn't accept her call to ministry until the year following. She was engaged in an official capacity three years later.

Lynn drove Connie places, for Connie was certainly "directionally challenged"! They vacationed together. They ate meals together. She was Connie's partner, servant, assistant, helper, and soul mate. Connie poured ministerial training into Lynn, as Lynn carried full-time responsibility as director of finance of the Genesee County Commission of Roads. Lynn never desired to pastor a church. Lynn was a background person, content being the person who allowed others to preach while Connie was "recovering."

Connie had been diagnosed with breast cancer the year before and had undergone all the required painful treatments. She had been declared "cancer free"! In December of 2002 she had come to Grand Rapids, where a community of women rejoiced with her as we celebrated how good she looked.

Two weeks later, she was hospitalized with cancer of the liver! For more than four weeks she stayed in the hospital undergoing intensive treatments. Lynn was there daily, most often on lunch hour to ensure that Connie would eat and drink. Connie's spouse, Ben, took the night shifts.

We all prayed. We all touched and agreed. We all spoke words of faith. We all claimed scripture. The congregation put the color green, symbolizing new life, all around her room. Constant praise music was played, for Connie was the queen of praise and worship!

One Friday evening her kidneys failed and they placed her in intensive care. And one week later, early on a Monday morning, Connie slipped into the gates of heaven with a smile on her face.

We were bereft, to say the least. This was not supposed to happen. Connie was one of our wise women. Connie was the center of many of our circles. Connie was an influential woman who made a significant impact everywhere she was present. Yet, we found ourselves without the physical Connie any longer. And life kept calling us to shift.

Lynn became the interim pastor. Ready or not! Pastoral leadership was thrust upon her. Following is part of the sermon that I preached at Lynn's request to Connie and Lynn's congregation the Sunday after Connie's funeral. Lynn had called, months prior, to book me while Connie was hospitalized. Lynn was simply trying to fill the pulpit. Neither of us knew that on the Monday before I was scheduled to preach, Connie would die. Her funeral was that Friday. I attended the funeral and stayed to preach on that Sunday.

IT'S TIME FOR A SHIFT!

There is a recent book on the market, entitled *Four Blind Mice*.[3] The author, Jack Patterson, is a white man who has really paid attention to the culture of our people. The chief character in this novel is a black man named Alex Cross. Alex has a Ph.D. Alex has three children. Alex works for the Washington, D.C., police department as an investigator and is always talking about quitting. His wife is dead. But his grandmother, whom we come to know as Nanny Mama, raised him and is now raising the children in his home.

I met Alex in the book *Roses are Red*. I followed him again in *Violets are Blue*. Both are engaging, entertaining, and interesting murder mysteries. Alex is a man who is always challenged. At the end of every book, he swears that he's had more than enough of the lifestyle of an inner city peace officer and that he's going to quit. Of course, he doesn't. For there is always another murder, another investigation, another challenge, and another book. For Alex is—as you and I are—the living testimony that good continues to overcome evil. Alex is, like all of us are, a witness that God will make a way.

When the road is rough . . . when the going is tough . . . when the hills are hard to climb—our God will show up. God shows up because we dare to wear the name Christian: one who is like Christ. We are those who have been redeemed by the blood of the Lamb. We are those who are the lights of the world. We are cities, set on a hill for nonbelievers to see, recognize, and come to know. Like Alex, all of us have another series of challenges. And we all have books to be written about our lives.

This modern day story salutes the memory of my sista-friend, Pastor Constance Wilkerson, and this woman pastor who walked beside her as a friend and a support, Pastor Lynn. I'm one black clergywoman who follows a pattern of scriptures to preach from each week. I don't pick and choose from what's on my mind. But I allow God to speak to me from the four preselected passages that most United Methodists, Catholics, Episcopalians, Lutherans, and Presbyterians will hear in their worship services. In this way, I can be in conversation with my friends around the country, about what they heard on any given Sunday.

When Rev. Lynn called to schedule this particular Sunday with me, because Pastor Connie was in the hospital, I looked at the four passages and had selected the words of the prophet Isaiah, chapter 43, verses 18–25, for our time together. It's a scripture about the comfort of God that is already on the way! I didn't know what this Sunday would hold for us, but God did!

Isaiah, the prophet, was not a man of high distinction. He was called by God to be the mouthpiece to a backsliding people. Isaiah was married to a prophetess and was a father of two sons. He seemed to be a quiet working man until the year that King Uzziah died and finally Isaiah saw the Lord. The Lord was high and lifted up and God's train filled the Temple. Uzziah was the king, but he was also a leper and his life expectancy was very short. He may have been a king, but lepers had no social life, for the disease was contagious. He may have been a king, but no one wanted to associate with him, get close to him, or be in his company. For lepers had to walk the earth, calling out, "Unclean. Unclean." It was a safety feature for the good of the whole community. Uzziah was king, but he was marked by death.

In the year that Uzziah died, Isaiah discovered that he, too, had an awful disease. He was shown his own sinfulness. He saw the ugliness of the people all around him. He found himself on the scales of justice before God, and Isaiah was found lacking.

He had been so focused on Uzziah before that he didn't deal with his own standing before the Almighty. He had been so caught up in the drama of the king, the court, and the community that he had not taken the time to look within. The distraction of the king had prevented him from seeing himself. So God had moved Uzziah and gotten Isaiah's attention.

Our dear friend's name was Constance. It was a regal name for a regal woman. Her name was Constance. It's an elaborate form of the words, "constant" or "consistent." Her name was comforter. Her name was classifier. Her name was celebrator. Her name was collaborator. Her name was sista. Her name was wife. Her name was mother. Her name was grandmother. Her name was pastor. Her name was friend. For she was the force of unity, togetherness, and community. She began a good work and named it Gate of Heaven. She role modeled how we are to pray and stay focused. She showed us how to live by the Word of God. She taught by precept and example how to walk the talk of faith. She was constant and consistent until God swept her through the gates of heaven on a bright Monday morning.

Pastor Connie now rests with the saints in glory. Surely, the hearts of those who loved her remain heavy, our spirits are yet grieved and certainly, our tears are not quite dry. But, on this Sunday, just two days after Connie's funeral, I have to help you, her congregation, understand that Connie is with God, who is calling all of us to shift into another gear.

For in this year that Pastor Connie has died, somebody has to see the Lord. In this year that Pastor Connie has died, somebody has to get the revelation that the pastoral mantle has been passed. In this year that Pastor Connie has died, somebody has to be the next witness, the next living testimony, the next package of seasoned salt to be poured out in the earthly realm for God.

The words of scripture in Isaiah 43, beginning at verse 18, are words of comfort to hurting people. The heading in some Bibles proclaims that this is a passage for when you are between a rock and a hard place. "Do not remember the former things, or consider the things of old. I am about to do a new thing; now it springs forth, do you not perceive it? I will make a way in the wilderness and rivers in the desert."

This is good news for the people of God who have been captured, enslaved, mistreated, and taken from their promised land. For forty chapters, representing many years and many different kings, Isaiah has called Israel to repent. He has called out warning after dire warning. But in chapter 40, God gives the prophet some good news to proclaim. God begins to speak comfort to the hurting, confused people of God. The days that are coming will be incomparable to the ones behind. It's time for a new day. It's time for a new beginning. For the foundation was laid well by Pastor Connie. But God has called a shift.

God called a shift for Pastor Connie. God said, "Well done, Servant Consistent. You have done all that you can do with a group of hard-headed, stiff-necked, and rebellious people. You have given them groundwork. You have fasted and prayed for them. You have been shepherd, mother, prodder, pusher, and puller of them. You have cried your last tear. You have prayed your last prayer. Shift Sista Constant to higher ground. Let's see now, what they can do for themselves? This is a test. What did we learn from the life and the witness of Pastor Constance?

She invested her final days in you. She prayed for you until the end. She tried to spare you hurt. She attempted to keep you from pain. She didn't want you to suffer on her regard. So, she kept quiet to keep you from worrying. And God told her to shift. Death is only a shifting from this life that we know into the one that we sing about so well. Death is the transition from life on earth to life eternal. But her death puts finality to what Pastor Connie can do now. Her name was Constance. It meant steadfast, unmovable, always abounding in truth, knowing that her labor was not in vain. For this is the Gate of Heaven and she's shown us how to get there. The question is: What will we do now?

God has already promised to make a way. We have the blessed assurance that Pastor Connie's legacy is not dead. Only her physical body is dead. What she gave to us, what she planted in us, the ways that she touched us live on in us. That is the seed that remains for you and for me to bring to good fruit. To the naked eye this is an awful day. It's only six days since Pastor Connie died. It's only been one day since we released her body back to the earth. Her beloved husband, Brother Ben, her family, the entire church family and all of us, her friends, are all yet reeling from the blow of her unexpected death. But we have come to talk about what God is requiring of us.

When a pastor dies usually the flock will scatter. Some will leave for other congregations. Some will go back to living their old lives. Some will simply fall away from organized religion and the fellowship of believers. If you think I'm confused, remember how the disciples went right back to fishing as soon as Jesus was killed. We have a reputation in the church for being flaky. Yet, God is saying let the past go. It's over. Release what was in order to move on.

When Lazarus came forth from the grave, it was after Jesus called him. Death had to turn the boy aloose. He came out of the grave yet wrapped in stinking grave cloths. Jesus looked at the crowd and said what? "Release him, and let him go." Jesus didn't call off the grave cloths. Jesus didn't walk over and pull on them. Jesus told the congregation, standing there weeping and wailing, unsure of what was happening, to move themselves to the place where they could do the work of shifting, in order to set the dead free! Freeing ourselves from dead stuff and dead people, even dead issues, is a fundamental leadership requirement. Old "dead" stuff, people, and issues soon begin to rot and to stink. As the primary Teacher, Jesus calls us to shift. "Release Connie and let her go!"

Setting Pastor Connie free is what God is calling each of us to do. Release the hold we have had on her ministry with us. Releasing it does not mean that we will forget her. Releasing her does not mean that we will never speak her name. Releasing her does not mean that we won't have an awesome, big picture of her hanging in whatever buildings we buy or build. But releasing her means that we will allow her spirit to rest in God's bosom. Releasing her means that we will commit to being as faithful to this ministry as we have been. Releasing her means that we will honor her investment in our life by remaining faithful, consistent, constant, and diligent to what God has called us to do. Saying good-bye to Pastor Connie will allow God to make a way for this ministry out of this wilderness of pain, hurt, and grief.

God says don't stay too long in yesterday, for deliverance and new hope are on the way. God has the plan already worked out. God has the devils tamed; the wild beasts have to honor the Almighty. For this is the Church of God, and God's name will be glorified. In God's Church there will always be a witness and a living testimony. In God's Church there will be rules for governing our lives, order in the way we behave, and morality in the way we live. For God is constant. God is consistent. God is omnipotent, omniscient, and omnipresent. There is no spot that God is not! The promise is even here, between this rock and this hard spot. God will make a way when we learn how to properly pray.

I've learned a lot about prayer with Connie's last illness. I don't know if you will confess or not, but often as I thought I was praying, I was really trying to convince God to follow my desires. I told God what to do, how to do it, got several people to touch and agree with me, and then waited on God to follow our directions. But Isaiah 43:22 says that I have really worked God's reserve nerve. For verse 22 declares, "Yet you did not call upon me, O Jacob; but you have been weary of me, O Israel!" Verse 24 finds God saying, "You have burdened me with your sins; you have wearied me with your iniquities." In prayer we come to God. In prayer we seek an audience with the Divine. In prayer we talk. But in prayer we also need to learn to listen. Prayer begins with praise and worship of the Almighty. Then prayer immediately moves into confession of our sin. How dare we presume to come before a holy God with junk, garbage, and ugliness in us? Confession opens the way for us to have an audience with the Sovereign.

After confession, we can offer our thanks for all that has been done already. Before we beg, let's try a bit of thanksgiving. Then, we can move into intercession for others, learning how to be constant as we stand before the throne with another's need in mind. We are admonished to pray for leaders all over the world. We are commissioned to pray for brothers and sisters on the journey. We are agents of prayer for those who don't know God in the pardon of their sin. All effective leaders have a developing prayer life.

Prayer is more than words. Prayer is sitting in quiet meditation. Prayer is lighting a candle and allowing the smoke to speak for you. Prayer is the tears that run down your face as words can't express your feelings. Prayer is reading the Word and allowing it to say what you can't articulate. Prayer is sitting quietly, singing, humming, and moaning songs. Prayer is admiring God's handiwork in nature, listening to the running water, and communing in your heart without words. Prayer is committing our will to the way of God. Prayer is surrender. Prayer is agreement that God really does know best and does have a better idea.

When it comes to the issues surrounding diversity, there is no place for human limitations. When it comes to moving ahead into the future that God has already designed, that the whole world be One Body, prayer openness is essential. For we have many "holds" on our thinking, placed there by our cultural conditioning. We have many "limits" around our boxes of "capacity building" when it comes to allowing others full access, full rights, and the full privilege of our group, our space, our team, and our congregation. A solid prayer life is the one place that the Holy Spirit can break into our spirit and enlarge our hearts to receive more, better, and even best.

Prayer is allowing the will of God to become our will. Isn't this what Jesus had to do in the Garden of Gethsamane? "It's not my will, but your will that is to be done." Jesus gave up the fight and allowed God to be in charge. Prayer is of course personal petition, taking our needs before God, yet trusting God enough to only say, "Bless me" and leaving the how, when, and where up to the one who loves us best. Finally, prayer is worship of God in our daily lives. It's more than the pious sounding words that we say. Prayer is our way of living on a day-by-day, consistent, and constant manner.

When we earnestly learn how to pray and to allow God to be God, then the promise is that our sins will be blotted out because of God's name. God longs to pardon us, to forgive us, to receive us back into fellowship, and to love us with an unconditional love all because we have taken on the name of Jesus Christ. God is constant in mercy, not giving us what we deserve. God is consistent in grace, giving us more than we can ever earn. God wants us to pray, in faith, believing so that we can be led out of this wilderness place and into the Gates of Heaven.

Release yesterday. Let go of what was. A new thing from God is on the way. Begin now to see the invisible, to believe the unimaginable, and to prepare for what seems impossible. For God has called a shift. The transition has begun. If we remain enslaved to the past, we will wither up and die. If we stay stuck in this place, between a rock and a hard spot, we cannot grow, mature, and be productive. If we remain stuck in what was, we will dishonor all that Pastor Constance lived, preached, prayed, and died for. For she was constant in calling us to grow up. She was consistent in telling us how to please God. She was steadfast in living as a faithful woman before us. Now, it's our turn. What will we do?

There are more than four blind mice among us. There are many of us who feel just like Alex Cross and want to call it quits! But we really do realize, understand, and sense that this is not the end. This is a new beginning. A new story starts, a new chapter will have to be written. The promise is if we sign on for this new shift, God has already promised to make a way. And I know the Lord will make a way, somehow.

Like the rose always knows how to be different than a lily; like the stars know not to try and twinkle during the day; like the trees know not to bud in the middle of a snowstorm, and like the birds know to fly south in winter and return in the spring, we can't explain it. Most of us don't have it figured out. But the same God who loved us so much that Jesus came, suffered, bled, died ,and rose again, is the same God who will lead us when we stop trying to dictate our direction and simply learn how to trust and to obey.

Look unto God, anticipating the new thing that is being created all around us. Can you see it? Can you sense it? Can you discern what God is requiring of you? Be still for a moment and listen with your whole heart. There is a shift in the air! Ready or not, it's here.

LET'S PAUSE AND BREATHE

1. What type of welfare system of God's is working best for you now?

2. When have you denied yourself availability of God's welfare plan through another?

3. Did you know that you were "welfare dependent"? When did you make this discovery?

4. How have you been part of God's welfare system for others?

5. Describe the last act of hospitality a sister extended to you?

6. Who or what are you grieving that needs to be "let go"?

7. What is the shift that God is requiring of you today?

_____

_____

_____

_____

_____

It is better to give than to receive . . . however, receiving is in God's plan too.

The Hebrew word shalom means hello, good-bye, and peace. When we say shalom, we are saying "peace" when we arrive and "peace" when we depart. We can take peace with us wherever we go. Peace is achieved one person at a time, through a series of friendships.

—Fatma Reda, *The Minnesota Press*

FIVE

THE SEASON OF LENT

WONDER IS A LONELY JOURNEY

"Your people will be my people"

There is a book on the market for little children. It's called *Are You My Mother?*[1] This book is about a little bird that falls out of the nest while its mother is away hunting food. This little bird gets lost, never having traveled before, and has sense enough to know that its mother would want to take care of it. So the little lost bird goes off seeking its mother.

It's a hilarious story. For the baby bird goes up to some strange objects, such as a bulldozer and a mail truck, and asks, "Are you my mother?" Now that might seem strange to us, but since the little bird had no frame of reference as to its identity and no mirrors to see what it looked like, the little bird inquired of anything and anyone. The little bird wanted to find out who was responsible for its care. The bird had a desire to discover to whom it belonged and where it lived. So, in its search to find a place called "home," the little bird was actually doing a series of eliminating those items that said "no." The little bird didn't stay around and try to fit in with those things that answered negatively. The bird continued to search for its authentic mother.

Of course there is a happy ending, as the mother bird finds the lost little one and carries it back to the nest and the family. But that searching for identity is played out in each one of us as we roam this planet earth. Until we find the place that claims us interiorly, takes us in with acceptance, welcomes us openly and makes us feel at home, we will wrestle with the complex issue of low self-esteem, wondering who we are. I would dare to say that the issue of low self-esteem is "the" key issue wreaking havoc in our lives!

Most of us don't know our spiritual gifts and our spiritual worth before God and we keep trying to do ministries and activities that don't fit us. We can't sing, but we'll ask the choir, "Are you my mother?" We can't arrive early enough to be a servant on the usher board, but we'll try to make that ministry our home. Some of us are too stingy, too cheap, and too parochial, but we will join the missions group and dare them to tell us that this is not the place that we belong.

The average one of us doesn't have the sense of that little bird that searched until it was found. For instead of leaving a group that has loudly said, "No! I am not your mother," and continuing on our search, we'll stay in a group that's a misfit and try our best to tear it up!

We have the same tendency in our personal lives. We try to make people accept us, when we know that we do not fit. We make attempts to force certain careers to make room for us, when we are miserable daily and making others sick of us. We want to be accepted by the right circles, live in the proper community, and drive the correct car. Yet, none of these things tells us who we really are. For the outer trappings might deceive others and often fool us too, but the outer stuff is simply superficial and transitory. The season of Lent calls each one of us to seriously go inward and identify who we are and who we belong to on the real side.

The forty days of Lent, not ever counting Sundays, allow us the opportunity to give due consideration to the fact that when Jesus comes again we had better know who we are. Do you remember the story of the five foolish virgins, each a woman of God? They got left behind while running around trying to find oil and the Bridegroom came and the doors were shut on them. When Jesus comes again there will not be time for any of us to run around and try to find our "lost selves." Jesus will come again, but as the Chief Shepherd, dividing sheep from goat. And he will be measuring out eternal rewards to those on the right side and eternal punishment to those who find themselves on the left. Do you know who you are?

A good role model for clarity of self-identification is our sister Ruth. Being kin to the little bird, Ruth wanted to belong to a group that she could identify with, have some relation to, and be comfortable with. Isn't this the big issue in every relationship of teamwork and leadership? Can I feel you? Can I relate to you? Can we talk the same language?

Yet as they stood at the crossroad, she had enough self-esteem, self-confidence, and self-assurance that she told Naomi, "Your people will be my people." This is a big statement. This is a huge jump. This is a leap of faith. For they had little in common with the exception of being females with a horrible past behind them!

An excellent lesson that Ruth teaches us is that we are more than enough all by ourselves! She gave Naomi a short, clear answer. She didn't try to impress her with her past accomplishment. She didn't give Naomi too much information about her plans for survival, that most likely she didn't have at hand right then! But she gave Naomi an answer directly and concisely, with impeccability. Short answers turn away wrath, says the Scriptures.

In this scene, Naomi was the senior woman with a history and a reputation. Yet, Ruth had the audacity to speak truth to Naomi's perceived power. Understand that people will always want to know your ace in the hole, but you don't have to tell them more than they need. This is another primary principal for women who are leaders. Learn how to give short, concise answers. Learn how not to give away too much information. Learn how to hear the questions that are asked. Respond appropriately with short answers.

SAVE YOUR SANITY, SOBRIETY, AND SOUL

Let's practice five necessary statements for the journey to Wonderful.

- "Yes."

- "No."

- "I resent that."

- "I don't appreciate that."

- And, finally, "I don't know."

These are short answers that won't give your power away. Ruth spoke with the authority of God as she gave her mother-in-law a short, clear, and impeccable answer that we continue to use in wedding ceremonies today.

This was a woman in a bad, even horrible situation. She had nothing tangible to offer. She had no kinfolk in Bethlehem to look to for assistance. She was a poor widow without a son to become her support. Yet the good news is that she knew exactly who she was and she had no qualms about self-identification. This is another impressive lesson that Ruth teaches us. People always do what they need to do for their own survival. It is not about you! Come on, you can say it. "Their stuff is not about me!"

In diversity issues, this is one of the best "self-talks" that we can provide for ourselves. For when diversity is the practice, stereotypes are the norm! People have all sorts of ideas, perceptions, notions, and thoughts about those who are different. But it is their stuff. We do best not to let it affect us internally. We can allow others to think whatever they think. Yet, we don't need to expend energy on their faulty thought life. Say it again. "Their stuff is not about me!"

Naomi was trying to save her own sanity. Naomi was desperate to retain her own sense of salvation in being a Jew. She was holding onto the last vestige of dignity she could muster by walking away from a dead past. So she named herself "Bitter Mara." She gave voice to the pain within herself and her limited outlook for another new beginning. But Ruth determined that this was not going to be her end. "Your people will be my people."

Holy Scriptures are universal! The Word of God has been preserved for the whole wide world. The world includes you and me. The good news of Ruth's leadership qualities in a multicultural situation speaks of you and me particularly. This means that it could be read like this: "There is no spot that God is not! And, wherever God is, I will be at home. There is no situation that is too hard for God. And, where God, is I am more than a conqueror! Wherever God is I belong, for I am a child of the Ancient of Days! And all of the people around me belong to The Most High God and we are family." This is who I am! This is who you are!

We end up in trouble when we allow others to name us. Names indicate how we act, behave, and respond. Folks, we end up real confused when we make attempts to fit where others want to place us. We find ourselves in a quandary when we cannot say for certain who we are. For the power to name is a gift from God. The power to claim our own identity with divinity is why Jesus came in the first place. Jesus came all the way from Glory, through forty-two borrowed wombs, including those of foreigners, Ruth and Rahab, in order to let us know that we are not simply dirt that is equivalent to about eighty cents when cremated. The pattern of multicultural relations is not a new twenty-first-century innovation!

We are not just African foreigners brought to the shores of the land of the free and home of the slaves to work for others. Our ancient forebears were leaders in math, medicine, science, and pharmaceutical discoveries. We are not the least, the last, and the neglected on everybody's list. Why, we built the pyramids that yet stand. We are not the sum total of our bills and charge account totals as we hurry up the educational, social, cultural, and economic ladders of life in a foreign land.

Thank God that we are not the alcoholics, the drug addicts, the sex hustlers, and the gangster rap that we portray in the Hollywood media. Thank God that we are not the welfare loving, ghetto living, head-rag wearing, nasty bandanna, broken tooth folks that television and the newspaper love to display when something goes down in the hood. Thank God that we are not the hoochie mamas, got lost daddy, baby having, baby makers that history has portrayed us as in classic educational text books!

Another powerful leadership lesson that we learn from Ruth is that she was not afraid to strike out into a new situation without all the props of her background and lineage. She was willing to leave her past in order to embrace an unknown future. This is the sign of a good leader. It's not the props that hold us up or together, it's the God-given call to lead others into Wonderful that resides deep within.

The people of Moab were in famine conditions. Their small gods were not providing food, nourishment, and water for them. The choice was to remain with them and face hard times and perhaps death, or face the rising sun of a new day to begin!

Ruth looked at Naomi and knew that Naomi thought she was a wild woman, a crazy upstart, and a nobody in Bethlehem. But Ruth had the inside scoop. Ruth had insider information. Ruth had the power of God working on the inside. She did not know that her spiritual gift was that of promoting the Jesus story with her womb. Yet she used the spiritual gifts of help, service, exhortation, and faith to perform her immediate task of witnessing her womanhood.

Her spiritual gifts put her outside the "normal" box. Her spiritual gifts had her coloring outside the lines. Her spiritual gifts had her appearing crazy to her mother-in-law, who didn't fully understand her own mission. But Ruth was clear: " I'm a whole person; wherever I am the Holy Spirit works on the inside of us, making positive changes on the outside for others to witness." The Holy Spirit takes the old, raw material that we bring and transforms us, makes us new, and gives us direction, clarity, and a bold voice. The Holy Spirit takes our fear and gives us blessed assurance. The Holy Spirit fills the aching void in our lives and raises our self-confidence, our self-esteem, and our self-worth. It is the power of the Holy Spirit that reminds us of why we were created in the first place. Our chief reason for existing is to tell others about the goodness of God.

Ruth knew that she had been "adopted" into a new family! By Jewish law she was in this family for life. She did not need her former clan, kinship group, or community to make her whole. She was so comfortable with herself that she was willing to go into a new place and make herself at home. She was so filled with a sense of who she was in the universe that tying herself to the old Ruth was no longer a possibility to consider.

With this statement of "Your people will be my people," Ruth entered the season of Lent. Yes, it would be lonely. Yes, it would make her uncomfortable. Yes, it would hurt to be in a place with strange customs, foods, values, and religious practices. Yes, she had much that had to die and be buried from the past. But she also had the fortitude of Naomi, who had made the journey to Moab some long years prior. If one woman has done it, we can do it too. This is the confidence of a leader. If no woman has ever accomplished what we have been chosen to do, still with God we are more than sufficient! This is the faith of a leader!

God knows that I enjoyed "meeting" leader Jill Nelson in her book *Straight, No Chaser!* Jill said:

> I want to write about black women to enable us to take voice, center stage, put us into the private and public dialogue which often has a devastating effect on our lives and from which we are usually excluded. I don't want to pimp black women because that would be the same as prostituting myself. I just want to get myself and my sisters into the discussion, join the fray. The singer Chaka Khan had a hit song in the early 1980s. The first line went, "I'm every woman, it's all in me." There's a collective consciousness among black women. It is not that we are all the same, just composed of many similar pieces, connected across class and age. I want to write about some of the crucial events in my own life as a way of identifying common threads in the lives of women, particularly black women. Once we've picked up those threads, I want to join the process of quilting, pulling those pieces together into whole cloth that will protect, shelter, and speak for us all.[2]

Jill is a seasoned writer who has worked for the *New York Times, Essence, USA Weekend,* and the *Village Voice.* She is a columnist for MSNBC Online and a hard hitter with words. She has faced the Lents of life. She has suffered all the various "isms." And she puts pen to paper about walking the journey in a diverse world.

> Sometimes I think the worst part of living in a culture entrenched in racism and racial hatred is the constant

wondering. Did I not get the job, was my call not returned, did the restaurant put me at the table next to the kitchen, pay me less, not include me, short-change me, did the police stop me, because I'm black? After a while, the wondering becomes as powerful as knowing. If you have a day in which you do not, overtly or covertly, encounter racism, you feel lucky. The sad truth is that sometimes it's enough that no one said or did anything negative to you; positive actions don't even figure into the equation. Even with a brief respite, you never really escape, since being a member of an easily identified and nationally loathed racial group seeps into your pores, gets in your blood stream and your psyche. Once the seed of black hatred is planted, it grows, fed with regularity by politicians, newspapers, magazines, television, pundits, casually and unthinkingly by the average white person on the street who either does not see you or sees you only as a threat . . .[3]

Ruth was walking the journey into an established culture that had these racist thoughts of her and those like her.

EXPECT TROUBLES AND ANTICIPATE MORE PROBLEMS

In the season of Lent bewilderment, detours, roadblocks, and stumbling blocks are all a part of the journey. We are walking with Jesus to Calvary. We are on a lonesome, solitary period of self-examination, reflection, and self-sacrifice. In this season Jesus faced rejection and betrayal. In this season Jesus was mocked and his friends ran away. In this season Jesus had to face the madness of his own people! He faced it with dignity, knowing that he was not alone. Not only did Jesus face the madness, he embraced it with a "Nevertheless, not my will but your will" attitude.

This is our purpose. This is our role. This is our function. This is our primary task. We are called to yield ourselves unto the call of God on our lives. We are to be so focused on our destiny that God can change our script, give us a new assignment, put us in foreign, diverse situations and take away all of our creature comforts, and we yet walk the talk! We can do it when we remember that it is only a passing season. "It came to pass . . . !" Nothing comes to stay forever; we will pass through it, moving on to Wonderful.

Beloved sista, the Middle Passage didn't take us out. Slavery didn't destroy us. Jim Crow didn't kill us. Sitting in the back of the bus only made us mad. We're like roaches, too strong for poor living conditions and mediocre foods to wipe out. We take rags and pieces of cloth to make designer clothing and head wraps. We will rap the equations to complex math; we will spiritualize our way out of danger; we will pat our feet to a gospel tune and take off up the rough side of the mountain. And when we hear Yolanda Adams, Cee Cee Winans, Albertina Walker, or Shirley Caesar, we will move on up a little higher and not even wonder about how we made it over! For the Holy Spirit in us keeps us alive and knowing, with clarity and certainty, that a brighter day and a new season is coming.

Lent is our season to self-actualize. This is our season to take another step toward our divine destiny. This is the season to know that some things, some places, and some issues have to die. In Lent that death is a sacrifice for our becoming more! Lent is another season to be like Ruth and to let the world know that "something within me holds the reins. Something within me banishes pain. Something within me, I cannot explain. But I'll let the world know that there is something within."[4]

It took Ruth years to come into a tiny inkling of her role in the lineage of Jesus Christ. Yet, she was able to say who she was at the crossroads. There was no identity question because she had found her place within the confines of Naomi's family. God was working out the plan of salvation. Jesus came. Jesus lived. Jesus died. Jesus rose again with victory. Jesus sent us the Holy Spirit. And Jesus is coming back again, for Ruth walked through her season of Lent into her destiny in Wonderful!

A CONTEMPORARY RUTH

I went to find an appropriate expression of both my support and my empathy for one of my sister-friends who has again encountered rejection. As I live, get older, and have more life experiences, I long for the day when this sort of demeaning behavior will cease and desist. It ain't happened yet! So, this book is written, in part, to offer both warning and methods to help us better deal with rejection in diverse situations. For into every life rejection will present itself. It's a big part of the journey experience.

Dr. Cathy Large is an African American woman who is self-assured, confident, bodacious, and quite well educated. Dr. Cathy Large has a Ph.D. in curriculum design and worked in this field for the local public school system until our former superintendent, Dr. Patricia Newby, retired.

Dr. Newby is a story in black female leadership all by herself. She was chosen to come to be our public school superintendent when the institution was on its failing last leg. She walked into the interview and every day there after wearing St. John knits! She is not what we call fair-skinned, but the sista came to town and kept her hair colored a high, light red. And she had the audacity to surround herself with both black and white, tenured, well-educated men and women to be her support staff. She brought Cathy into the central building to work with her in an administrative post.

After five years of being ridiculed, mocked, and publicly humiliated, weekly, by the town news media, at one fine and public school board meeting, the very proper, in charge, and in control Dr. Newby shocked the entire board by announcing her retirement at the end of the school year. She had taken matters into her own hands and walked off into a new future despite all the hoopla. The startled board replaced her with a nice, gentle, soft-speaking and smiling white male. The savior had come!

It was after Dr. Newby's retirement that Cathy was replaced by a woman with a Master's degree in music. Can you believe this? Talk about a slap in the face. Talk about big time rejection. Talk about insult and humiliation. We can now talk about the fact that when we look at this scene closely, it's not a new one. It's racism with a different face. But all of us are not deceived with this subtlety, hidden beneath a quiet smiling face that is working diligently to make the school system more palatable to a wider community whose children are in private and "Christian" schools.

Since I have had similar experiences, I was able to share with Sista Cathy some of the lessons that I've had to learn. They were not "new" lessons, but some of the very same ones that Naomi and Ruth role modeled for us. As Christians, we "ought" to know that we are in line for "repeat." It won't be nice, easy, or fun. But if they rejected Jesus, who in the world are we to expect to slide by free? Certainly Jesus knew this reality, for "He came unto his own. And his own received him not" (John 1:11).

A primary lesson that I learned is found in the card that I sent to Cathy. It's a Maya Angelou *Life Mosaic* from Hallmark. Mother Maya put this on a bookmark for Cathy to keep: "I can be changed by what happens to me. I refuse to be reduced by it." The card goes on to read: "In the face of such uncertainty, believe in these two things—you are stronger than you think, and you are not alone." We must learn how to believe in God, in ourselves, and in the power of community. For none of us is ever alone This is truly good news in hard times. Naomi had Ruth. Ruth had Naomi. They were community.

The second primary lesson that I learned was that, sometimes, those we "see" as our enemies are really angels in disguise. Lot and his family lived in a foreign community that was filled with evil (another biblically diverse situation). And we know that evil is ubiquitous. But there is no spot that God is not looking out for us and intending for all of us to just get along. So when things got out of hand in Lot's town, in Ruth and Naomi's town, in my town, in your town, and in Cathy's, God sends angels to escort us to the mountains, the high places where no devastation can occur!

Lot didn't recognize the angels. Lot was not personally acquainted with the angels sent. Yet the angels got them out of a situation that was doomed and saved Lot's life and that of his family. Get the message, folks. Public schools everywhere are in imminent danger, regardless of who is at the helm The public schools are not simply an educational issue but an economic and political issue as well.

Primary lesson number three that I learned was that angels come in so many different shapes, sizes, and colors (as we now know from the television show *Touched by an Angel*). Those we think are our enemies can often come to us with good words that will eventually save our lives and those of many others. This is not to say that these "angels" mean us well. This is not to idealize evil intent. Rather, this is to help us remember that "what they meant for evil, God meant for good for the saving of many lives" (Gen. 50:20). This comes from the story of Joseph, sold into slavery by his jealous brothers. The Bible also goes on to record that God has even used a jackass in order to save a good person's life. (I know for certain that God continues to use jackasses!)

Sometimes we are so fixated on where we are, we don't recognize that God is calling us to pack up and move to better. I never appreciate being rejected. I hate that Cathy had to experience this humiliation so publicly too. But this is the Jesus way, right? They took him out to a public garbage dump and hung him high. The good news is that, despite all their rejection, God raised him up. Sista Cathy walked through her Lent, for she knew that Easter is always on the way. We are resurrection people and getting up is our constant theme of praise!

LET'S PAUSE AND BREATHE

1. What parts of your past history is God calling for you to let die and be buried?
2. Who are the people that God is calling for you to walk away from so that your journey to Wonderful is not obscured?
3. Name the places where you are the sole individual who looks like you?
4. How do you make these situations work for your advantage?
5. When was the last time that you were both the teacher and the lesson for cultural diversity?
6. What is your role in the telling of the Jesus story?
7. Name your primary spiritual gifts.
8. Have you taken a gift discovery questionnaire? If not, find a copy of *Spiritual Gifts Can Make Your Church Grow*. It's an Upper Room book by John Bryant. It has the Holt's Modified Questionnaire in the rear and will help you discover where you fit in the Body of Christ.

I have discovered that:

_____

_____

_____

_____

_____

_____

_____

_____

Now is the time for black women to reflect constructively upon their place and work in the church. Their thinking is constructive when it holds leadership accountable for its moral posture in the church and community. . . . Female critical thinking yields discourse and actions that relieve the church of provincial denominational politics supporting patriarchy and prohibiting joint economic planning . . ."

— Delores S. Williams, *Embracing the Spirit*

SIX

THE SEASON OF EASTER

WONDER WISE!

Your God will be my God"

After school, we waited to hear Mom call, "Come on, it's time to eat." That sound rounded up my seven siblings and my father. It was her welcome to a table set with delicious, homemade foods and bread. But before we could take our seat, there was another question to be answered: "Did you wash up?" For you could not be ready for dinner if your face and hands were not clean. The other nine folks could be prepared to say grace, but they might have to wait, hungry and anxious, if another hadn't washed up. The ritual for meal times was set around a family table. We came to eat, gave God thanks for the Bread of Life, as well as the food before us. Then we ate together.

We ate "family style" where food was passed from one to another. Mother always served my father's plate first. Then the food was passed around to the children, and Mom ate last. More often than not there were plenty of vegetables and homemade bread for seconds. I loved the smell, the taste, and the availability of fresh breads. Mother was an excellent cook. She'd had good preparation from Big Mama.

Big Mama had moved north from Mississippi, where ample meals with fresh bread were the norm. I can remember watching the process for making potato rolls. The peeling, dicing, boiling, mashing through a sieve, and adding to flour, yeast, sugar, butter, milk, and salt was a complicated process that took too long and got your hands messy. I never mastered the art! Big Mama was a deaconness at our church. She was responsible for making the communion bread. She made it without yeast and rolled it flat. It smelled like rolls and, with a bit of extra butter, brown sugar and cinnamon, became a childhood treat. When served at church, broken into little, "sacred" pieces and offered as "the Body of Christ, broken for you," I never got enough. The pieces were too small.

Bread was a staple in our large family. If bread was available, there was a way to feed hungry children. Hot biscuits or cornbread muffins loaded with butter, and even biscuits made with raisins and frosting on top would stave off hunger pangs and serve as a treat. I can remember going home at lunch time and mother would take biscuit dough and cook it in a skillet, on top of the stove. Talk about good. As the oldest girl in the family, I learned to make most of these different breads. But I never learned to make rolls or loaves of bread. I felt that this was a special "right" reserved for the matriarchs.

I believed that if I learned how to do their role, they would die. Now, I know that's silly, for they both died and I can't make their potato rolls today! But as a young girl, I knew I needed them to stay close and provide some measure of protection for me. I remember the ritual of gathering around the family table. I remember the loving care that went into the women's planning and preparing food. I remember the sacred time of giving God thanks for the food that we were about to eat. I remember the rules about hands and face having to be clean. I can remember the anger of those who had to wait for the one who was sent back to wash up. And I remember the tension around our table.

I remember trying to eat fast in order to get away from that awful environment. I remember stuffing bread in my pockets, so that after being excused from the table, I could eat in peace. My father was an abusive tyrant. My mother was a woman who had been moved from Mississippi in order to live with a childless aunt and uncle. She felt abandoned and rejected by her mother and brothers. She needed to feel love. For too many years my mother endured my father's emotional abuse.

Our family table was not a happy place. We all sat in fear of what names we would be called, what new punishments might be directed our way, or what answer to a question might incur my fathers's always available wrath. I always hoped it would be different, but it never was.

Yet, I have grown to love communion at the family table. I was prepared by Mom to be ready when the call "Come on, it's time to eat" was made. The metaphor for "washing up" speaks to me about doing what is necessary to gather with "the family" at this meal Jesus Christ has prepared.

THERE IS ANOTHER FAMILY TABLE

The season of Lent calls me to check my thoughts and my motives. Lent requires that I consider how I am using my body and my time for God. Lent reminds me that the family of God is waiting for me to come and eat. And Easter tells me that the Bread is done! The Lord's table is different from my memories of home. This is a table prepared by a loving host who graciously gave his body and his blood at Calvary to ensure that I have more than enough food for my journey. At this table, I am affirmed. I am encouraged. I am strengthened. I hear soft and gentle words and I experience tender care. With this sharing, at a family table, thanks is offered and protection provided. I'm never in a hurry to leave. If I choose, I can linger in the presence of Love who rose on Easter!

Easter is about getting up. Easter is about rising above the death of dreams and hopes. Easter is about the ability to come back stronger than those who felt they had constructed our demise! Easter says that Fridays—with pain, hurt, and humiliation—will come, but just wait until Easter morning! Easter says that evil does not have the last word. Easter says that God in Christ rose in triumph over sin, death, and hell. Easter says that Ruth and I standing at our crossroads chose the life-giving, life-sustaining, and the life-giving God.

Ruth told Naomi, "Your God will be my God." She and Naomi were headed towards Bethlehem, the city of bread. Although a famine had driven Naomi and her spouse from there years before, life had written a new script. Now, with the famine in Moab, the women were set to head towards Wonderful. Naomi felt that she was going backwards! Ruth didn't know where she was headed, but was ready to go. Neither one of them realized that they were part of the serving team for the Bread of the world! But that woman named Wisdom directed their steps away from all of their past mistakes, misfortunes, and seeming failures toward their divine destiny.

Brenda Lane Richardson and Dr. Brenda Wade wrote *What Mama Couldn't Tell Us about Love: Healing the Emotional Legacy of Slavery, Celebrating Our Light*. They provide for us primary lessons about our "emotional inheritance."

They list seven anti-intimacy beliefs:

1. There will never be enough of anything that I need, especially love.
2. I'm not good enough to be loved.
3. I'll lose anyone who gets close to me.
4. It's not safe for me to face my anger.
5. No matter what I do, it won't make a difference.
6. I have to control everyone and everything around me to protect myself from being hurt again.
7. My body is not my own.

Then, they provide us with seven life enhancing beliefs that we can begin to internalize:

1. God loves me!
2. I can make something from nothing!
3. I can make a way where there seems to be no way!
4. My heart will guide me if I listen!

5. I bring humor and joy to my life!
6. I can inspire others to achieve!
7. My friends are my sisters![1]

They conclude that, "Accustomed to forging 'sisterly close' relationships, we can use our notion of extended family to create support groups, help one another to grow, and introduce one another to prospective mates . . . when we pay attention to the signal system of our 'feelings,' we can make congruent, reality-oriented decisions about our lives."[2] This is woman's wisdom at its best.

Wisdom is a woman, according to the ancient book of Proverbs. In Proverbs 1, we are introduced to her call to all who will listen and heed her words of counsel. By Proverbs 8, we find that she was present at the creation, dancing and rejoicing by God's side. Wisdom is the principle thing to grasp as we journey toward our destiny. This woman called Wisdom is easily accessible and ready to journey with us all the way. She is God's ultimate instructor of community leadership.

Thanks be unto God that she helped Ruth to select the right God. All the little gods, Ruth left behind in her past. She looked forward with anticipation and upward with hope in the Sovereign One. She was determined that she and Naomi were going to find Bread!

The Bread, with its smells, symbols, metaphors, and memories, is presented and broken into pieces that represent the broken body of Jesus for our sin. As the crust is broken, never cut, and the crumbs fly everywhere, I can see both Naomi and Ruth, Mama and Big Mama, mixing, kneading, rolling, and making their offerings of love. Now that it is my privilege to call the family, "Come on, it's time to eat," I tell them to take a big piece of the Bread, for I know there is more than enough for all. And we all need big portions of the Bread as we journey to Wonderful!

A CONTEMPORARY RUTH

Her name is Darlene. That's short for "darling." And a darling friend is she! I met her when Mista Chuck and I were looking for a house. Darlene is a real estate agent who helped us find our home. It was a difficult experience, as I knew "exactly" what I wanted. I had all my "needs, desires, and wants" written on the back of an envelope! She had to work from this detailed list as we went searching.

Riding in her car, I noticed that every time we would pass a Catholic Church, she would do the sign of the cross and apologize. It was her way of acknowledging the God of her faith. And she wanted me and anyone else to know exactly how strongly she felt about her faith.

Darlene is the third daughter of a middle-class family, born and raised in Oklahoma. Her father was in the military, stationed in San Antonio, Texas, as she was growing up. Tomboy that she was, Darlene stayed in trouble. Her mother became very concerned and decided that she needed the firm hand of her father to corral her energy. They found a boarding school in San Antonio and Darlene found herself enrolled in an all-girls' school.

The Order of the Sisters of the Holy Ghost was home of a group of German nuns. Darlene was not very happy at being away from home and its more open environments, and she was not thrilled at being in an all-girls' school. The school at "home" was all African American and she knew her way around the campus, the community, and challenges of school with two older sisters. She was in the eighth grade. She was just entering her teens. She was in the stage of development where identity was important. Being a "good" girl was not at the forefront of her agenda.

She begin to assert her leadership skills among her new peers. She had them skipping classes, jumping out of windows to go into town, raiding refrigerators, and doing the kind of activities that had her sent to San Antonio in the first place. Leaders lead. And, in this multicultural setting, Darlene was leading other "good" girls astray. Enter the German nun Sista Boniface! Stern, but compassionate. Rigid, but caring. A stickler for rules, but one to know how to stretch some boundaries. White, but yearning to know the young Darlene.

Sister Boniface did not push rules and regulations into the young woman's face. Sister Boniface did not threaten to reject her and send her home. Sister Boniface realized the leadership potential within Darlene and begin to introduce her to another leader, whose name was Jesus Christ. Sister Boniface allowed the power of the Holy Ghost to give her discernment, wisdom, and the ability to feed a young woman with the Living Bread of Life.

Darlene began to see her activities in the light of "hurting" the One who had given his life for her. Darlene became appreciative of the love that Christ offered her through a strange-looking Anglo woman who wore the full vestment of black gown, hood, and shoes. She was hungry for an identity and discovered her Christian formation and foundations in the Order of the Sisters of the Holy Ghost and Sister Boniface.

Eighth grade was a turning point in her life. This was a pivotal year in the life of a young, searching woman who found a place at a huge table and began to eat of the community that she experienced. Darlene was "rescued" the next year and sent to another boarding school closer to her mom and sisters. But in the tenth grade she and Sister Boniface reconnected at the school in San Antonio. The changes in her faith formation continued.

Darlene is quick to tell you that she has experienced some painful lessons while growing up. She gave her parents the "fits" that they had tried to avoid! Even into her adult years, like all of us, she did some things that she would not like to have advertised. But the early stages of her living faith, which she attributes to Sister Boniface, have always drawn her back to the Church of Jesus Christ.

Like her mentor, Darlene is stern but compassionate. She is a gift-giving woman who reaches out to touch others with the Bread of Life that sustains her. Darlene is a stickler for rules; she helped to start the Red Hat Group in our town that does not allow members under fifty. Yet she was quick to say that "younger women" could attend, but they had to wear "pink" hats! And, like Sister Boniface, Darlene's leadership abilities stretch across racial, ethnic, and class lines as she is led by the Holy Spirit in assisting others to find houses to make their homes.

Darlene does not limit her involvement to simply "sales." She is invested in so many community events that make a difference in the lives of others. She gives of her time, her gifts, and her energies to contribute her piece of "Bread" to the larger table of communion. For taking in the Body of Christ demands that she become an imitator of the One whose name she bears as a Christian.

Sister Boniface walked the journey with a young African American girl who was lost and didn't know her way. This German nun was willing to take her by her hands and spoon feed her until she was able to feed herself and all the others that God has allowed her life to touch. Darlene's parents and one sister have died. Yet Sister Boniface introduced Darlene to a family that is worldwide and inclusive. She will never be alone in the Catholic Church.

Darlene found our home for us with that list on the rear of the envelope. When I arrived at her office that morning, worn from the searching, she had a big smile on her face. "Linda, I have found 'the' house. And I've already made sure that your mortgage approval is secure." By the time that Mista Chuck got to see the house that evening, after work, it was a done deal! The Bread of Heaven had prepared a table for us, and Darlene had been our server!

I thought that when we closed on our home, our relationship was finished too. Little did I know that Darlene follows up on her clients! She had already contributed many decorating ideas as we had searched. She came to our open house celebration bearing a house-warming gift. She sends us holiday and "just because" cards. I recognize that this is all part of good sales details, but with Darlene it is also an investment into our well-being.

Darlene just happened to "drop by" to say hello when I was wrestling with a huge decision about where to locate my business. As I engaged her in conversation about my new search, she provided wise counsel and accurate discernment, and acted as an "angel" with good words of business wisdom. She has given me an "Angel of the Spirit" that sits in my office, right in front of my computer. It reminds me that whenever Darlene passes a Catholic church building and crosses herself, she is praying for me.

All of us who know, love, and work with Darlene give God praise and thanks for Darlene Eaves, who embodies every memory and every imitation of Sister Boniface. Their mutual journey continues to feed our hungry spirits and calls us to deeper communion and community with each other!

LET'S PAUSE AND BREATHE

1. Whenever we sit down with another to break bread it is communion. How do you give thanks for the Bread of life in public gatherings?

2. What is the symbol of "family gatherings" for you?

3. How does your family share meals today?

4. Describe your thoughts around the communion event at your house of worship.

5. How do you personally prepare yourself to receive the Lord's Supper?

6. Did it ever occur to you that on the night Jesus was betrayed he served as a mother, by washing the disciples feet? Then he played the father, the host, by giving God thanks for the meal before serving it? What does the mother image, the nurturing Jesus, do for you?

7. Who helped you to discover that the table of Jesus Christ had a place set for you?

8. How does the Ruth declaration of choosing the right God fit you today? Are there small gods in your life that are preventing your journey to Wonderful? Name those gods.

_____

_____

_____

_____

_____

The only thing wrong with failing or making a mistake is to not learn its lesson! "Women are blessed with a jewel of strength that glows all the time!

—Judith Jamison

SEVEN

THE SEASON OF PENTECOST

WONDER-FILLED!

"This is my covenant with God"

Stumbling blocks can turn into stepping stones. For God has already ordered our steps. The story of Ruth involves three primary characters: Naomi, a bitter woman on the edge of desolation, filled with despair; Ruth, a foreign woman going to make her home in the Jewish culture where she will be called "that gentile"; and Boaz, the kinsman-redeemer, who represents Jesus Christ in this story, the adult son of a prostitute. All of these individuals have the perfect right to feel alone, abandoned, rejected, and miserable. Each one of them qualifies for any of the drugs that we take to keep our mental balance. Each one of them had major issues! Yet God had a grand plan involving three seeming misfits.

In the season of Pentecost, Jesus sends the Holy Spirit into the Upper Room where a group of misfits are hidden together, praying and waiting. God has this thing with using those who don't have a chance in the politically correct order of the world. God has this knack for piecing together lives that seem to have been discarded, junked, and even thrown away to make them into vessels of honor. The Holy Spirit blew into a room where the scared had been having "scared and very quiet church" and touched them, sat upon them, kissed them, filled them with power, and then sent them into the streets to announce good news to the whole world. Sound like the story of Naomi, Ruth, and Boaz?

We have no word of why Boaz had never married. We have no knowledge of his inner feelings toward life without a wife or sons. We have no record of how he attained the great wealth that he had accumulated. But we know that he was a miracle waiting to happen. We know that he was a leader among men. We know that he was wealthy and had vast holdings. And we know that God had a great plan for his life.

We don't know how Ruth discovered where his fields were located. Nor do we discover how or when Ruth learned about the Jewish custom of leaving some grain in the field for those who had nothing. Perhaps Naomi had taught Ruth the lesson of providing for those who are poorer in Moab. Maybe they talked about this tradition along their journey. However, we know that the culture of Jerusalem demanded that those who owned fields did not glean everything for themselves. So we find Ruth asking Naomi if she could go into the harvest fields with those others who were forced to glean or pick up the deliberate "leftovers." Naomi said, "Go, my daughter!"

"Go" sounds like such a little word. "Go" seems like such a small step to take. "Go" does not appear to have miracles, marvels, and mystery all packed within. But "go" is a word that is pregnant with possibilities. "Go" allows a search for the new and the different. "Go" permits another step towards destiny and Wonderful. "Go" lets the mind take flight and the imagination churn. Naomi said, "Go." Ruth took off for fields unknown and "found" Boaz! The Chinese say that the journey of a thousand miles begins with the first step! Our "leader," Sista Ruth, was yet stepping toward her destiny.

These two widows had arrived in Bethlehem between the months of March and May, which was the barley season. Thanks be unto God, every field had to leave something for the "gleaners." Usually gleaners were the poor, the alien, and the widowed.

Leaders are known for going among the "common and ordinary" people, learning how they accomplish their task in order to show them ways and methods to do it better. Ruth had no hesitation about hard work. Ruth was not afraid of entering a place where she was not known or welcomed ahead of time. She was a risk taker. She made herself vulnerable. She dared to move out of her comfort zone and into the wider world in order to learn how to conduct business.

Ruth found herself in a place where God had a miracle awaiting her action of work. Seemingly by chance, Ruth "wanders" into the fields of a wealthy man who has wonderful relationships with his hired hands. The psalmist declares, "The steps of the righteous are ordered by the Lord" (Psa. 37:23). It was no mere accident that Ruth was in the right place to find God's divine favor as well as food. The timing of God is providential.

Boaz was of the family of Elimelech, Naomi's dead spouse. Boaz didn't know it, but destiny was about to overtake him in the place that he thought he owned. Sometimes the very thing we are looking for is in our possession all the time. Sometimes we are so busy looking far away that we miss the miracle of Love that is right in our face! Sometimes we simply don't recognize God, who is everywhere at the same time.

"Where you die," said Ruth to Naomi, "I will die. And, there I will be buried." This was a covenant between two women. This was a verbal contract that made Ruth responsible for providing for her mother-in-law. With these words fresh upon her mind, Ruth left to seek life! She went into the fields of Boaz and found favor with the reapers. They begin to drop grain in her path on purpose! Ruth was determined that neither she nor Naomi would ever be hungry again. The favor of God made provision for them both because she dared to "go."

Every challenge in our lives has within it the potential for wonder and divine favor. Every situation that comes to trip us up, take away our faith, and shake our confidence in God has the seed of promise buried within it. Before Ruth was born she was in the plan of God. While she was a young girl playing make believe, God had her destiny in mind. When she married into the family of Elimelech and Naomi, it was no accident. Her destiny was in divine order. And, as she became a widow and had to suffer a broken heart, God was there all the time.

My sista-friend, Dr. Sheron C. Patterson, senior pastor of St. Paul United Methodist Church in Dallas, is the creator of the Love Clinic, which helps women to grow into sisterhood and self-love. She is the author of several books and is on the national circuit telling her "truth." In her most recent book, *New Faith: A Black Christian Woman's Guide to Reformation, Re-Creation, Rediscovery, Renaissance, Resurrection, and Revival,* she addresses our sisters, Ruth and Naomi.

> New Faith forces us to embrace every woman as our sister, because we cannot have a future without each other. No longer are we competition. Our faith in God is more powerful than our outer characteristics. New Faith tells us where we went wrong and with the snap of a hand points the right way to go. Does it matter if her skin is as dark as charcoal or fair as the snow? Does it matter if her nose is a wide as a freeway or narrow like a rural pathway? Why do we dwell on the outside, my sister. Your potential friend is not composed of nostrils or melanin but the soul. We must have soul sisters. Our souls require each other."
>
> . . . There is no mistaking a sister. We must cultivate adoration for us and be our own safe places and nesting niches. We can no longer afford to be at odds over anything—a man, a job or money. In the name of New Faith, I call a cease-fire. Desist from all cat fights, name-calling, finger-pointing. New Faith declares that we are all on the same side: there are no enemies here. New Faith taught me that if I love Jesus, then I love me, and I must love my sister. It is a natural progression of love.[1]

She goes on to clarify:

Before we can start pledging like Ruth and Naomi, we take these steps.

1. Exhale any negatives. Forgive whatever somebody did or did not do.

2. Rehearse in your mind the good deeds by our fore-mothers—Clara Hale, Rosa Parks, Fannie Lou Hamer. The sister you are meeting may be the next heroine.

3. Alter your attitude. Hold your neck, if need be; keep it from working involuntarily. Try not to jump to con-clusions when you think someone is disrespecting you. The sister may base her reaction on yours. Be the role model for her.

4. Speak to each other in love. Monitor the tone of your voice.

5. Smile. Make eye contract. This sister is you.

6. Create your own safe places.

7. Pray for each other. Lift up each other in daily talk with God . . .[2]

Sheron concludes with these words of wisdom: "Sisters every-where need your prayers. . . . With your sisters locked in step with you, nothing is impossible. A chorus of us–heads thrown back, voices piercing the sky—is awesome. Your sisters will keep you marching. Their energy will propel you forward when you are weary. Their shoulders will prop you up when you are sad. Their eyes are your spotlights. Their backs are your bridge."[3]

CHEERLEADERS NEEDED

When Naomi tried to send Ruth back to her parents, it was God who cheered her on towards making a new decision. As she stood at the crossroads, Wisdom put a steel rod in her back, clapped her hands, and pushed her past the point of no return! Now, in the Land of Bread, God put her in a position where she was looked upon with kindness, with grace, and with favor by those who didn't even know her personally. For her destiny was evolving. God's Spirit was weaving together all the strands of this group of misfit and broken lives into a wonderful and wonder-filled new tapestry, a new story and another beginning!

FRESH OIL AND NEW WIND

As the Holy Spirit arrives on the day of Pentecost there is a shift and a change in the atmosphere. As the Holy Spirit comes blowing into the room, kissing and touching, the anointing of God begins to bestow favor upon a group of misfits. The anointing means those who are touched by God. The anointing is a sign of the Holy Spirit's presence and power. The Anointed One is Jesus Christ, who also came touching, calling, healing, feeding, forgiving, and caring for the least, the last, and the lost. When Jesus Christ returned to heaven, the Holy Spirit was sent to touch with favor and power those in the Upper Room. Then they were told, like Ruth, to "go!"

The paradigm shifted and those who had been bashful and scared became bold and outgoing. Those who had been hidden ran down the stairs into the street and took authority in the center of the city. Those who had been whispering began to shout out the good news. Those who had been afraid for their lives, intimidated by the threat of death, decided to live for someone whose name was Jesus Christ!

In Bethlehem, the paradigm shifted and the foreign woman became a bold leader and the bitter woman found renewing hope creeping back into her heart. The name Ruth is most likely a contraction of *reuth*, which is the Hebrew word used for "the act of seeing" or "sight." That she was a woman of vision we have already discovered. She now "sees" that it is time to go and find food for she and Naomi. As she fulfills her covenant vow, God provides favor.

Favor is the pleasure of God that smiles upon us for our obedience. Favor is that extra measure of grace that God gives to those chosen. Favor is that benefit that we cannot earn. When Boaz noticed the foreign woman in his fields, he asked his laborers about her. Discovering that she was the daughter-in-law of Naomi, he instructed them to drop extra sheaves on her behalf. When he introduced himself to her, she was invited to make his field her "regular" field for gleaning. This was nothing but favor!

A woman without the support of a male would be an easy target for workers to take advantage of at any time. Boaz offered Ruth a protected place. The Almighty had given her shelter under the watchful eyes of a kinsman-redeemer that she did not even know. Ruth was blown away by this unexpected favor, kindness, and charity shown to her. A benefactor who was generous in spite of her being an outsider was almost too good to believe. She hurried to tell Naomi of their good fortune. The psalmist says that God's loving kindness is better than life!

On her first day seeking work and food, Ruth ran smack dab into her future! Boaz was a wealthy man. He was a kind man. He was a generous man. And he was attracted to a foreign woman. In Wonderful there is such a thing as a rags-to-riches story. In Wonderful you can find yourself moving from poverty to plenty, from being empty to being in a state of overflow!

Watching Bishop T. D. Jakes on television early one Sunday morning, I heard him preaching of the favor of God upon Ruth. He declared, "Favor ain't fair!" Favor is simply God's uncommon blessing that is not expected, not anticipated, and not looked for in life. Favor is the smile of God upon our life when the chips are down. Favor is about doors being opened, ways being made, and Red Seas having to part in our lives when we thought we were both down and out!

Amazing grace is our receiving what we don't deserve from an awesome God. Mercy is being kept from reaping what we so justly deserve. And favor is the extra that God throws in without explanation or good reason. I agree that favor ain't fair! It's just the overflow of the abundant goodness of a kind God. I'm sure that Ruth didn't care about "fairness" on that day. She was simply grateful for finding an abundant harvest to carry home.

HOW TO FIND WONDERFUL

When she discovered how well Ruth was gleaning in the fields of their relative Boaz, Naomi told her daughter-in-law how to set a well-intentioned trap for the brother. In chapter 3, verses 3 and 4, we find these words: "Now wash and anoint yourself, and put on your best clothes and go down to the threshing floor; but do not make yourself known to the man until he has finished eating and drinking. When he lies down, observe the place where he lies; then, go and uncover his feet and lie down; and he will tell you what to do."

Girlfriend, this is wisdom at its best! In the worst of times, when it seems as if your life is going down the tube, when your confidence is shaky and you don't know who or where to turn to for help, get dressed up and look good! For you don't know when destiny is going to smack you in the face! Get yourself a wonder-ful outfit. Find the nearest consignment shop if necessary and get a good bargain. Scrimp, save, or borrow some good cologne. Get ready to step out and meet your future.

It doesn't sound like "saved and sanctified" advice! It is not very pious language. But Mother Naomi told Ruth to make herself available to Boaz. To uncover a man's feet was the common language regarding the act of having sex. So what Naomi said to Ruth was get ready for action of the intimate sort. It's about availability. They didn't "do it." For Boaz respected Ruth and her position as a caregiver for his kinswoman. But he knew from her appearance, her wonderful, fresh smell, and her actions that Sista was ready and available.

Instead of taking advantage of Ruth, Boaz took her request of "spread your cloak over your servant, for you are next-of-kin" (3:9) as her bodacious way to ask for marriage and relief from her barren and widowed state. Boaz was not insulted. Boaz was not in-timidated by a strong, forceful woman. Boaz pronounced a bless-ing upon Ruth: "The Lord bless you, my daughter."

A BLESSING

The "blessing" invoked in this period was not like our politically correct, "God bless you" that usually passes for a pious "hello." The blessing that Jews greeted each other with meant that they were releasing a divine benefit from God upon you and yours. The blessing that Jews gave anticipated something wonderful happen-ing in and for the life of the one being blessed. The blessing that Jews prayed for one another was a gracious prayer for all of God's beneficence to be rained upon the one prayed for. The blessing was not a passive statement but an active one! The blessing means that all of the resources of heaven are at our disposal for gifting to another.

Boaz declared to a foreign woman that the God who created the heavens and the earth was going to increase her future because she had acted on her faith in Naomi's God. She was in the right place. She was in the season of ingathering. She had met the right man. It was Wonderful!

Boaz realized that life was about to change for him too. By her making herself available to him, an older man without children, she had just opened a myriad of pregnant possibilities for his future too. Talk about a happy camper in a multicultural situation! With all the rules that had to be tended to, with all the talk that their marriage would cause and with all the mixing of cultures that they would have to overcome, life was moving in Wonderful.

To be available to the Holy Spirit's movement in our life is the call of this chapter. The season of Pentecost comes to find us in our places of fear and to draw us out into the world with a message of salvation and hope. To be in the mental, emotional, and spiritual state of readiness to "go" and be a witness for Jesus Christ is to receive power for the task before us. The Holy Spirit longs to touch and anoint us, to be present in and to us, to work on our behalf and to provide what we need before we even ask.

HOLY, BODACIOUS, AND VIRTUOUS

When Boaz awakened and found Ruth lying at his feet, everything in him rose to the occasion. He found himself startled but wanting to protect her reputation. He told her that he was not the closest relative to Naomi, but there was one ahead of him as kinsman-redeemer. He had Ruth leave before dawn to ensure that no one would see her and smear her good name. He told her "do not to be afraid . . . for all the assembly of my people know that you are a worthy [virtuous] woman (3:11).

The word "virtuous" in Hebrew does not mean one who is pious, meek, and weak. It is really a compound phrase, *ischar chayil*, meaning one of strong force. So everyone in Bethlehem knew that Ruth was a woman of strong force! She was someone to be reckoned with and she was the one taking care of Naomi. She didn't depend upon her own strength, wisdom, or resources but followed an older woman's sage advice and was holy, bodacious, and virtuous!

The benefit of being available that early morning and of being a woman of strong force, stating her need with boldness, was that Boaz filled up her shawl with barley. Ruth didn't have to glean. She didn't have to stoop over for leftovers in the field. She was given more than enough by the owner, Naomi's kinsman-redeemer! They were in the town of Wonderful!

CONTEMPORARY RUTHS

They are the ebony and the ivory on the piano. They are the hotdog and the bun, the cookie and the milk as well as the coffee and the cream. They complement each other. They can complete each other's statements. They have a mixed "marriage" and they love, honor, and respect each other. It's a business "marriage" that they have and it didn't begin very smoothly.

One was trained as a social worker. She lived all of her life in the inner city and had much urban wit. The other one lived in the suburbs and owned her own floral business that she really loved but disliked that she worked alone. She wanted to change careers before age forty. The social worker decided to move into a new phase of her life. The suburban woman decided to seek new relationships in community—life in the city. They were both mothers and had needs to meet and to satisfy.

They were both go-getters. They were both ambitious. They were both bold and steadfast in their commitment to excellence. One was a typical type A perfectionist. The other is really laid back, cool but with an eye for the above-standard method. They are both creative and energetic. They met and disliked each other upon meeting. Yet they needed each other in order to make a successful new beginning as they pursued a journey to Wonderful.

This is the story of women in leadership, helping each other to succeed. Victoria Upton, Queen of the Universe, attended a seminar for women seeking to become entrepreneurs, a seminar supported by the Small Business Administrations (SBA) local office and administered by GROW (Grand Rapids Opportunities for Women). Vicki, a bodacious African American sista, decided to birth a magazine for women and she named her "baby" *Woman's Lifestyle*. It was introduced to the world in April 1998.

The U.S. Small Business Administration's Office of Women's Business Ownership (OWBO) is the only office in the federal government established to help women become full partners in economic development through small business ownership. OWBO provides programs across our country that support women entrepreneurs from business start-up to expansion through a variety of services and resources. Women anywhere can log onto the OWBO home page at: http://www.sbaonline.sba.gov/womeninbusiness. All SBA programs are extended to the public on a nondiscriminatory basis. It's worth exploring. It gave *Woman's Lifestyle* a leg to stand upon at its conception.

Woman's Lifestyle is about fifty-six pages of joyous education. The mission statement says: "Our mission is to provide women with information that is essential, enlightening and entertaining and to provide our advertisers with high quality service and an effective advertising medium. Our content is resourceful and sincere. We strive to maintain a high level of integrity as a positive, inspiring and progressive presence in our community." As a trained and skilled social worker, Vicki was sick and tired of all the things that can depress, delay, and deny a woman's joy. She is committed to the sisterhood's best.

Roxanne O'Neil, a "neat" Anglo woman, answered Vicki's ad for a sales manager. It was not love at first sight! As a matter of fact, Vicki told Rox straight out, "You can't do what I need." Roxanne heard challenge in that statement! Roxanne felt immediate anger as a response. And Roxanne determined that she was going to prove the Queen of the Universe wrong! A relationship was born that continues today. Both these women demand excellence. Both of these women are dedicated to educating women to become their best. Both of these women pull some very long hours every week until the magazine has been put to bed.

Ms. Ebony and Ms. Ivory have stories that they can share about the journey of working together, trying various concepts, taking each other through stormy life situations and holding each other's hands, wiping each other's eyes and simply crying together as sisters on the journey.

The magazine has a publisher: Victoria Upton. Editor in chief and business writer is Maureen Radlick, Goddess of Creative Inspiration—June Cleaver. Layout artists are Charice Andrea and Wilma Flintstone. Health Writer is Robyn Hubbard, M.D. Book reviewer and feature writer is Alexandria M. Fix. Beauty guru is

Marianne Bockheim. Lifestyle writer is Jan Deremo Forrest, volunteer connection is Esther, advertising sales manager is Roxanne O'Neil, and salesperson is Rae Gehringer.

There is a host of contributing writers who make the news magazine for women happen, including Terry Bienkowski, Nichole Thieda, Melissa Powell Sheppard, Anne Marie Cox, Dawn Ulmer Morrison, Kathleen Bowen Piggins, Jana Ortiz, Debbie Lea, Brandle Valenzuela, Mary Turner, and Angela Klinske.

Their office is in the suite across the hall from mine. I can testify to the countless ways, methods, strategies, and tricks that this group will accomplish to make women feel important, dream impossible dreams, stay encouraged, become better informed, and desire to move to the next level. They turn over rocks, walk tall buildings, go beneath the gutters, and rise to every occasion, seeking the multiple avenues that uplift the story of women on the move.

Ms. Ebony is the creative dynamo. The magazine is a work of art. The stories speak volumes about factual information, and yet, Vicki makes "her baby" seem close to magical, whimsical, and entertaining. She is the person primarily behind the scenes, sitting quietly at the computer. Mrs. Ivory is the individual answering the door, talking on the phone, going to get in your face to get your ad, your story, and your money. Together, they make it work so that it appears effortless—that is, until towards the end of the month when deadlines are tight. Like the keys on the piano, they work together and make beautiful notes of harmony.

Both Vicki and Rox are mentors in the community. Each summer interns are brought in to learn "how to do it" the best way possible. They are a part of the movers and shakers in our community who make things happen! Every community ought to have a *Woman's Lifestyle* magazine. For it tells our stories, lists our joys, champions our causes, and lets us see other women, like ourselves, who dare to be on their way to Wonderful!

LET'S PAUSE AND BREATHE

The journey upward, to Wonderful, is filled with many twists and turns. The roads are not straight. The valleys are deep and the hills are high. Sometimes we need to stop for a bit of refreshment.

What are the types of practices and rituals that help you to refresh, regroup, and become recharged on the journey?

_____

_____

_____

1. What is it that you need to be bold about and speak the truth about that demands a favorable answer?
2. Who is it that you need to serve as your mentor, your collaborator, or your clarifier for this season?
3. For what purpose do you need a "cover," a protector, a person who is able to assist your forward movement?
4. Where are the places that you are gleaning in this season?

_____

_____

_____

_____

Many different shapes and forms of candles may be found in your local stores. Catholics continue to use candles as they pray for another's soul. It is helpful to allow the smoke of the candle to speak to God on your own behalf. For Romans 8 says that we don't know how to pray for ourselves anyway! So find a quiet spot, put on some wordless music, light the candles, and allow the Holy Spirit to pray for you with the smoke! Honest, it's alright!

There is a spirit song that vibrates within us—a song we can sing without words—it is the song of the soul, the something within us that connects us to our source. When we allow ourselves to be a channel for that source of divine love and inspiration, God creates through us and the work is not hard. We are open to wider worlds, and we hear songs waiting to be sung, dances asking to be choreographed, pots wanting to be shaped, patterns asking to be quilted through willing hands that are open and receptive. Then the work of creating is not a labor. It flows through us and the words of Jesus resonate through our gifts—'My yoke is easy, and my burden is light'"(Matt. 11:30).

—Bishop Beverly J. Shamana, *Seeing in the Dark*

EIGHT

THE SEASON OF ORDINARY TIMES

WONDERFUL!

"Nothing will separate us"

I t's all about the power of the bloodline. There was a man in Bethlehem who was related to Elimelech. He was Naomi's next of kin. Kinship meant something significant in the Jewish culture. This relative was obligated to do something about the widow of his blood relationships. The laws of Moses made it his responsibility to provide for Naomi. There was property involved, land with value. This nameless man had first right to purchase it, farm it, and keep the proceeds as well as accept Ruth as a wife. Blood ties families together. There are many family quarrels and separations, but bloodlines last. Bloodlines can be traced for generations. Nothing can separate blood!

When Boaz awoke and discovered Ruth lying at his feet, he recognized that she had made herself available to become his wife. Being an honorable man, he told her that he must first go and see if the man with first rights wanted to "buy the property" of which she is part and parcel. So Boaz went to the elders who sat at the gate and called a meeting with the kinsman-redeemer to ask him if he would "do the right thing" by Elimelech.

The waiting time had to have been horrible. There can be no explanation as to the thoughts, ideas, and wondering of a woman who waited to see whose wife she would become! There is no imaging the ideas that went through the mind of Ruth as she went over the vow she had made to Naomi that had gotten her into this situation of "wait and see." Her mother-in-law told her, "Wait, my daughter, until you learn how the matter turns out; for the man will not rest, but will settle the matter today" (3:18).

There is something about sitting still that is troublesome. There is something about active waiting that is difficult to do. There is something about not knowing that brings uncertainty to our mind. Yet we are told, like Ruth, "Be still, and know that I am God" (Psa. 46:10).

To be still does not mean to confine oneself to a chair, a couch, or the bed and recline. To be still does not mean that we cease the necessary activities that fill our day. To be still means that we cease worry, stop fidgeting, and release the anxiety by relaxing, releasing, and letting go with deep cleansing breathes. To be still is to completely hand the matter over to God and trust that all things will work together for our good. To be still is an act of faith in the promises of God. To be still is to rest in God's love, God's history, and God's unfailing Word.

ORDINARY BLESSINGS

"Be still while the kinsman-redeemer works it out for our wholeness" is what Naomi told Ruth. "Stop worrying while the kinsman-redeemer is working," is what the mother-in-law said to her daughter-in-law, with confidence in Boaz. "We are in good hands with the right man on our side" is what wise Naomi told a perplexed Ruth. For the kinsman-redeemer had risen up from the threshing floor and immediately gone to resolve the issue of "who gets Ruth as his wife?" His actions said that nothing was going to separate him from Ruth, and Naomi knew it.

In her work *God Don't Like Ugly: African American Women Handing on Spiritual Values*, homiletics professor Theresa L. Fry Brown addresses the extended family concept.

Bridging the gap of who to be at home and who to be in the world proved difficult for blacks in general and black youth in particular. Few black youth . . . could afford to go 'seeking the meaning of life' like many of their white counterparts . . . they faced discrimination and tried to find their place in society through endurance and at times, protest. Even when in jail many received the message that their families would always be there for them. Their 'extended families' were responsible for providing love and assurance to help them face the adversities of life.

The black extended family is a multi-generational, interdependent kinship system. It is welded together by a sense of obligation to relatives. It is centered in a family-based household and is guided by a dominant family figure. The black extended family household reaches across geographical boundaries and can be both a moral and financial and economic support for several generations of relatives. It is the place where leadership, security, sense of true family, group direction, and personal identity evolve and are reinforced.[1]

She goes on to explain that

The family base is generally the home of the dominant family member, often the grandparents. It is the place of large family activities such as reunions and holidays, and times of family celebrations, sorrow and in crisis. In two or three generations the sub-extended family (nuclear unit) may become extended units of themselves . . . the dominant family member in most African American families provides leadership either through assumption or appointment . . . although it is clear that family members must be able to stand up for themselves, be self-sufficient, work and go to school, family members turn to this person in times of need—such as when they need temporary shelter, economic support, or interim child care. The dominant family member spends energy keeping the family together, exemplifying familial closeness, love, and concern. He or she helps socialize children, passes down family history, conveys heritage, teaches skills and techniques of survival, helps regulate the moral behavior of the family members, upholds the family spiritual life, and keeps individual and collective family secrets. Part of the power ascribed to the dominant family member comes through awareness of the burdens and concerns of the family.[2]

Fry Brown concludes, "The position of the dominant family member is similar to that of a charismatic leader in a larger social context. He or she has unquestioned authority and is the source of wisdom and law."[3] Time brought Boaz to this exalted role. It was an anticipated position. It was an acceptable expectation. This was his season! And it was all so very Wonderful!

ORDINARY SEASON

This is the season of ordinary time. It's the season between Pentecost and the beginning of Advent. It is the longest season of the Christian year, when there are no festivals, pageants, or celebrations built around the person of Jesus Christ. In this season the altar color is green for growth and growing. In this season we are to live by our faith. We are to gather and rehearse our shared faith story. In this season we are to covenant that nothing will separate us from the love of God in Christ Jesus.

In this long ordinary season we are kept by the power of the saving blood, the atoning work of Jesus, and the power of the Holy Spirit, as we wait with confidence. We walk daily, by our faith. We sing, daily, the songs that build our confidence. We share, daily, with one another and pray for each other. And we know that our kinsman-redeemer is taking care of our daily business as we are being faithful to take care of his Church. Boaz took care of the "redemption" matter, while Naomi and Ruth continued on with their daily life. In the same way we trust the faithfulness of God in the ordinary and mundane days of our lives.

The nameless kinsman-redeemer who was the closest kin to Elimelech refused to purchase the land. He wanted nothing to do with the land, for it included Naomi, Ruth, and any children that

Ruth would have. The children would be considered the offspring of Ruth's dead husband, and the land would revert back upon a male child's adulthood. This was the law of the levirate system. This was the rule that kept a woman in a family despite her first husband's death. The widow was passed down the line to brothers or other male relatives as property. Can you imagine being passed down the line of male relatives of your spouse or significant other? Makes you sort of ill, doesn't it?

To redeem a person means that you buy back the object that will make them whole again. To redeem a person means that you will give them another opportunity to be restored, revived, and renewed. To redeem a person means that they are made right before the world. Jesus, our elder brother, redeemed us with his own precious and atoning blood!

THE KINSMAN-REDEEMER

The symbol of the kinsman-redeemer in the book of Ruth shows us how God established a Jesus prototype in earlier generations. The nameless male who had a chance to be in the Jesus story backed out of history. "I cannot redeem it for myself without damaging my own inheritance. Take my right of redemption yourself, for I cannot redeem it" (4:7–10). He was not the leader for this season.

Boaz accepted the offer to become the leader, the man of authority, the one responsible, a person who was next of kin. It is written that he said to the elders at the gate: "Today you are witnesses that I have acquired from the hand of Naomi all that belonged to Elimelech and all that belonged to Chilion and Mahlon. I have also acquired Ruth the Moabite, the wife of Mahlon, to be my wife, to maintain the dead man's name on his inheritance, in order that the name of the dead may not be cut off from his kindred and from the gate of his native place; today you are witnesses" (4:8–10).

Ruth had made a decision, back at the crossroads in Moab, to let nothing separate her from her mother-in-law. She had kept her word and walked with her into a new and foreign land. She had gone to work and made provision for their daily bread. And, now, it seemed as if the vow at the crossroads had paid off in an unexpected way.

Life had thrown a curve ball at Ruth. Life had tried to take her out for the count. Life had shifted the ground rules, giving her a different and very difficult part to play. But, the blood line that connected Mahlon to his mother was deep enough that Ruth accepted the challenge to do what a dead son could not do. Blessings often come from unexpected sources. Blessings often come from unanticipated people. And blessings often overtake us when we are faithful to God in the difficulties of our lives!

Boaz stepped up to the plate and accepted Ruth as his wife and redeemed Naomi from a life of bitterness. Boaz took responsibility for Naomi, Ruth, and Mahlon and by so doing stepped into the Jesus bloodline! Boaz went above and beyond what Naomi or Ruth had thought or imagined, but our God is the God of exceedingly above what we ask, think, or imagine! Boaz, the son of a prostitute, married a foreigner, a woman from a bad place like Moab, and became the great-grandfather of David, the greatest king in Israel. It's all about the blood.

> God smiled upon the marriage of honorable Boaz and virtuous Ruth, and blessed them with a son whom they named Obed that means "a servant who worships." As Ruth was the servant who came to worship Jehovah, we can imagine her son's name as being expressive of her own conversion from idolatry. Through the birth of Obed, who became the father of Jesse, who was the father of King David, Ruth found herself numbered among the elect, and God wove the thread of her life most intricately into the web of history both before and after Christ. . . . It was from Boaz, an Israelite without guile, and from Ruth, who became an Israelite, not in race, but in mind, not in blood but in faith; not by tribe but by virtue and goodness that Jesus came as the most perfect expression of all graces.[4]

In Matthew 1:5, as we look at the genealogy of Jesus Christ, we find that Boaz was the son of Rahab, the harlot who saved the ten spies from Israel! It's pretty strange that the blood of a harlot, a woman who sold herself for a living, and the blood of a foreign woman, Ruth, intermingled to help produce a legacy for Jesus to come through. The Jews didn't want to admit a Moabite man into their kinship group, but God slipped a Moabite woman, a harmless looking woman, right in on them and they were happy for Boaz!

In the church of my childhood we sang a song that I'm not sure has an author or even a written tune. But, the words are so fresh with me today, "I'll let nothing separate me from God's love! I'll let nothing separate me from God's love! Through hard trials, tribulations, persecutions, I'll be faithful. For, I'll let nothing separate me from God's love!"

Powerful words. Powerful vow. Powerful truth when you understand the meaning of being connected and covered by the blood of Jesus Christ. Ruth had no knowledge of a Jesus when she made covenant with Naomi. But, it took her vow to get Jesus here! It's all about the bloodlines! Nothing can separate us from the blood!

A CONTEMPORARY RUTH

Are you following your vision?

Folks who wait until night to have a dream miss so very much. The world has told us, even taught us, that we are not to daydream. You can be called foolish, not bright, and even stupid when you can sit in a spot and not be fully present.

Daydreamers are those who dare to go off into another world. Daydreamers are those who see what cannot be touched. Daydreamers are those who slip into the unseen world and come back with something that the world needs to see! God continues to speak to those who are ready to receive daydreams. We can even call some of them visions.

Visionary people are right-brain, creative individuals. Their lives are not staid, dull, or normal. They see something and work diligently to make it real, solid, and current. Visionaries lead lives of excitement, fatigue, and shakiness. For all the things they "see" cannot be put into words. Concepts, ideas, and dreams are not always simple to explain. Bringing the unseen, the undone, and the unexplainable to life requires risk taking.

I remember distinctly one day doing something that I'd "seen" in a vision but, of course, had never done before, when I cried out to God, "I feel as if I'm walking on Jell-O!" And, the Still Voice responded, "A life of faith is walking on Jell-O!"

One day, at lunch with Sister Barbara Hansen, OP, I listened to the story of a visionary group of women who have done and are doing things they have never done before. One of Barb's housemates, Sister Kay Oosdyke, OP, is forced to travel to Chicago for teaching assignments. She's a gifted woman with a Ph.D. in theology who lives in Grand Rapids. One would think that with all of our colleges and universities, work would be plentiful. However, she is a female. And she is a nun. Could that be her problem? Mmmmmm . . .

Or it could be that God gave her a mission and she had to follow "the heavenly vision" (Acts 26:19)? On the streets of Chicago's Southside, Sister Kay saw a young African American mother walking down the street with a heavy load of laundry and three small children. It was a sight that snatched her attention.

She pulled over and made an attempt to offer the woman and children a ride. After much persuasion, they got into the car and Sister Kay took them to the laundry and a new relationship was forged. It was more than a ride. It was the beginning of a vision to make things better for this single mom. Visions have the tendency to grow and to spread. Visions catch up others and pull them along.

Over the holidays, the three young black children and their two additional siblings were the guest of four white nuns. They wanted the mother to have a respite. They wanted to give her a break. They wanted her to experience some downtime, alone. So Sister Kay brought all five young guests. The oldest was ten, and there was an eight-year-old, a set of twins, and an infant in diapers.

Can you see this crew of all white nuns and five black children? I told Barb that we needed to make a movie of them, trying to keep up with this group. It must have been an exhausting experience. But, it would make a super *Sister Act 3*!

These are four women who have never been married. These are four women who took a vow of chastity to forgo the opportunity to ever have babies from their own wombs. These are four women who had visions years ago that they could serve God best by serving all of God's children. Now they are aging. And, yet, for a week they changed baby diapers! Periodically, they continue this loving practice. They dared to be obedient to Sister Kay's vision of taking a journey with a young woman so unlike herself! They love both Kay and the children and the children view them as "family." It's all about the blood of Jesus Christ that unites us across ethnic and racial lines.

The oldest child, a wise young woman, said during the visit, "Sister Kay, people are looking at us strange!" Isn't she observant? For Kay, Barb, Sister Jude Bloch, OP, and Sister Sue Tracy, OP, their other sisters in the Order of Preaching Nuns, are mixing and mingling and taking care of those who don't look like them. They are not their kind? Or are they?

Conversion and new birth makes us all one. We can journey together although we are different on the outside. This has been a lesson I've had to deal with and learn over and over again on my way to Wonderful. I was forced to discover and to agree that God's vision has always been for an inclusive family. This includes all of us. Whoever Christ did not die for is excluded from heavenly visions. Now, we all have to deal with this truth!

LET'S PAUSE AND BREATHE

1. What "Land of Wait" does God have you in currently?
2. What are the different methods of "waiting" that work for you?
3. Who has God placed in your life recently to take on the role of a "kinsman-redeemer" when you were in need?
4. How did this "ordinary blessing" come into your life?
5. What is "green and growing" in your spiritual life presently?
6. Name several "strange-strained" blood relationships in your family lineage. What "good" can you imagine to bless them with today?

Every Woman!

Every woman should know how to live alone . . . even if she
doesn't like it.

Every woman should know whom she can trust, whom she can't,
and why she shouldn't take it personally.

Every woman should know where to go . . . be it to her best
friend's table or a charming inn in the woods when her soul
needs soothing.

Every woman should know what she can and can't accomplish in
a day, a month, and a year.

Every woman should have one old love she can imagine going
back to and one who reminds her of just how far she has
come.

Every woman should have enough money within her control to
move out and rent a place on her own, even if she never
wants to or needs to.

Every woman should have something perfect to wear if the
employer or date of her dreams wants to see her in an hour.

Every woman should have a youth she's content to leave behind.

Every woman should have a past juicy enough that she's looking
forward to retelling it in her old age.

Every woman should have a set of screwdrivers, a cordless drill,
and a black lace bra.

Every woman should have one friend who always makes her
laugh and one who lets her cry.

Every woman should have a good piece of furniture not previously owned by anyone else in her family.

Every woman should have eight matching plates, wine glasses with stems, and a recipe for a meal that will make her guests feel honored.

Every woman should have a feeling of control over her destiny.

Every woman should know how to fall in love without losing herself, how to quit a job, how to break up with a lover, and how to confront a friend without ruining the friendship.

Every woman should know when to try harder and when to walk away.

Every woman should know that she can't change the length of her calves, the width of her hips, or the nature of her parents.

Every woman should know that her childhood may not have been perfect . . . but it's over!

Every woman should know what she would and wouldn't do for love or more.

Every woman should know herself!

—Anonymous (from the e-mail circuit)

No black woman can become an intellectual without decolonizing her mind.

—bell hooks

NINE

IT'S THE SEASON
OF ADVENT AGAIN

WONDERFUL GRACE!

"She is better to you than seven sons"

Remember the tale of Ms. Chicken (a.k.a. the Little Red Hen) told in chapter 3? Although Ms. Chicken asked the other barnyard animals repeatedly for help, she ended up bringing in the harvest alone. She planted the seed, watered it, weeded the plants, gathered the grain, carted it to the mill, ground it, and baked the resulting bread all by herself.

Then guess which lazy barnyard animals showed up at her door wanting to share in the feast of the luscious-smelling rolls and bread? Guess who wanted to claim the harvest she had worked so hard for?

To whom does the harvest belong? Who can honestly say that "I helped with the labor?" Who can declare with sincerity, "I did my part?" Where are the women who have made it their business to help search for and bring new souls to God? Where are the sista-girls who have sacrificed to ensure that the land, the building, the sanctuary is always clean and in order? Where are the bodacious sisters who do evangelism, home visits, counseling, and intercession without being begged or babied to do their part? Who are the bold and courageous girlfriends who call out the weeds, the troublemakers, the lazy, the hypocrites, the slick, and the manipulative? For if we have not been diligent workers, there will be no harvest for us!

I'm sure that we are all acquainted with the ministry of stewardship. I'm well aware that most of us have been "churched" long enough to know that we are to do outreach to our community. The community needs to know that we are some praying, teaching, preaching, giving women. The community ought have evidence to our commitment to the youth, to the seniors, to the wayward, and to the hurting. The community to which we belong should be assured that if there's work to be done, they can depend upon seeing our faces somewhere in the place! For Ruth has taught us well, by example, that there is going to be a harvest and she was determined to get her share!

She made the journey well. She kept her vow. She used the gifts at her disposal. She was a leader. She was a risk taker. She made herself both vulnerable and available. She worked. She was blessed with divine favor. She found a good man who married her. She made herself "at home" in a multicultural community. She was received, accepted, and affirmed by the women of that community. Then she conceived a son. She carried that child. She labored to bring that child into the world. And the village "mothers" took her child, named him, and claimed him for Naomi! Ruth found herself on another journey!

After all Ruth had achieved to reach Wonderful and to discover her destiny, she was both blessed and then dismissed! The village prayed for Boaz: "May the Lord make the woman who is coming into your house like Rachel and Leah, who together built up the house of Israel. May you produce children in Ephrathah and bestow a name in Bethlehem; and, through the children that the Lord will give you by this young woman, may your house be like the house of Perez, whom Tamar bore to Judah" (4:11–12).

Their prayer recounts the significance of the wombs of other women who have dared to risk doing "the impossible" and the "never been done this way before" methods to continue the lineage of the tribe of Judah. They pulled in Rachel who was loved and Leah who was despised by Jacob. They spoke highly of Tamar, who set a trap and had sex with her father-in-law, Judah, to bring Perez into the world. Where Naomi had never publicly acknowledged Ruth's reclaiming of a life for her, the people of the village heralded her as a heroine. They spoke her into Jewish visibility and acceptance. Often the recognition we deserve does not come from those we have worked with and for so diligently. But God has a way of making our destiny known publicly!

Yet the season in Wonderful is not forever! The season in Wonderful is only a respite. Yes! Even our season in Wonderful has to die so a new season will come. It is the way of life in the Spirit. Ruth had the baby. Boaz was the father. But the story takes us right back to Naomi, who had named herself "Bitter Mara." Isn't it strange that this woman who had convinced herself that life was over for her, found herself with a newborn and a supportive community?

Once again the journey of Advent called this trio. The misfits had been forged together with a bloodline called and blessed by God. Their lives had been woven into a beautiful and complex pattern. Naomi had to learn how to live again. Ruth had to learn how to become part of an accepting new village, a new and embracing culture, and a brand new role, that of mother! Boaz, at his age, had to learn how to become the head of a different household with an aged relative and a newborn child. The Advent of new themes were just beginning. This was not the end of a story. It was only another beginning! They had made history and it was time to begin all over again.

It's awesome to recognize that Ruth indeed had a good and prosperous harvest. She played the role of Ms. Chicken very well. We never hear Naomi's audible thanks for her toil and labors. But we get the high praise of Ruth from the community "wise women." They declared that she was indeed better to Naomi than seven sons! That was quite a compliment. For sons were the ideal gender. Girls were simply tolerated. One son could have saved Naomi from the journey back to Bethlehem. But, though she had lost her sons, she was now more than wealthy, she was blessed beyond words. She got the infant, Obed. Ruth got the accolades. Everybody got a new Advent!

"In the final ironic moment, Ruth—whose language and actions sought to incorporate Naomi into her new family—is erased from the text. Her mother-in-law nurses the child, the local women name him, and they even proclaim, 'A son has been born to Naomi' (4:17). This erasure removes the child from any Moabite stigma. Confirming this pure pedigree is the genealogy with which the book concludes . . . And Ruth, the ostensible heroine of the story, is left an enigma; her continuing relationship to Naomi, her feelings for her son and husband, and her sense of belonging in Israel are never addressed."[1] Truly Ruth is at another crossroads. The journey begins again!

For every blessing also comes with its own pain! With every hello there is a good-bye. With every good-bye there is a hello. Author Dorothy Bryant says it this way: "Like an old gold-panning prospector, you must resign yourself to digging up a lot of sand from which you will later patiently wash out a few minute particles of gold ore."[2] "No one and no one thing, is good all the time. . . . if we expect nothing but gold, we are distorting life, getting in our own way."[3] Ruth had arrived in Wonderful and life was preparing to change and to challenge her again!

HARVEST READY

Mark 4:3 finds Jesus saying, "Listen! A sower went out to sow. And as he sowed, some seed fell on the path, and the birds came and ate it up." This means that either we, as pastors, or those who serve as our pastors, sow the Word of God every time the doors are open. Pastors are charged before God to have a Word that is just for the hungry. Many of us will come to hear it, but as soon as the worship is over, we go away to do the same old things we did before worship began.

Then, there are "seed(s) [that fall] on rocky ground" (Mark 4:4). These are those folks who hop from place to place seeking the latest thrill. They don't have any root in Jesus Christ, they just want a place to express emotions. They want to do right, but when trouble comes their way, they go back to doing the same old thing that brought relief the last time.

Some of us are like "seed [that falls] among thorns, and the thorns grew up and choked it and it yielded no gain" (Mark 4:7). These are those who join the church to see how much they can hustle. For the church can be a good hustle. They are deceived by what money represents and don't understand that if you have Christ, money will find you.

But there are those folks who are like Ms. Chicken and Ruth! The seed falls upon good ground. It comes up, grows and produces a harvest that multiplies thirty, sixty, or even a hundred times. I want that hundredfold harvest, don't you? As a matter of fact, if you look at Deuteronomy 1:11, Moses prays for the people of God and says, "May the Lord, the God of your ancestors, increase you a thousand times more and bless you, as [God] has promised you!" All we have to do is help with the work of Jesus Christ.

We are not called to do it all. We are not called to do it alone. We are called to community and gifted by the Holy Spirit to work together to present ourselves to the world as a soul saving station. We all have to do our parts. Jesus paid the full price for the land on Calvary. He sent the Holy Spirit to assist us in the plowing, planting, weeding, and in-gathering. We each have a part to play. We cannot stand around looking, like those barnyard animals. For the summer is past. The fruit, vegetables, and grain fields are ready for harvest. The laborers are few. The question as we stand at the crossroad is: Who will go and help little Ms. Chicken?

God has already made provision for the harvest again this year. In the beginning, the law of reproduction was sown into all the creation. Farmers will bring in the fruit of their labor again this year. It's another "ordinary" reminder that there is much work to be done in order for us to celebrate a harvest. None of us can sit down and declare, "It's all over!" For the work begins again to ensure another crop and harvest.

The night before he was betrayed, Jesus shared a meal with his friends. He offered them bread after giving God thanks for it. The bread was for the little child in each one of us, for Jesus wants us to come like children. The little children were so loved by Jesus.

And every little child needs company along the journey. For it is mandated that the little child will one day soon take others by the hands and lead them into the fields of labor we have cultivated for the realm of God.

Jesus gave his friends wine. The grape juice that we drink represents the blood Jesus shed for each one of us with human skin. The color of our skin makes no difference. The Bread, the body of our Savior, and the grape juice, the fruit of the vine that represents the blood of our next-of-kin, remind us that Jesus left heaven to come down to earth to offer us his divinity. Each of us has a spark of the divine within us—that *imago dei* that Ruth discovered at the crossroads.

It's a Wonderful story! It's a Wonderful life! And every season of our life holds the potential for being Wonderful! For each day presents us with new beginnings, new possibilities, and new opportunities to encounter our destiny and to become what God has dreamed for us. God's dream for us is so much bigger than we have ever imagined. In John 14:12 Jesus tells us that we would do "greater works" than he did while he was on earth. But too often fear keeps us majoring in minor issues, forgetting that we are called to perform "greater works!"

Ruth and Naomi have blessed my life, my ministry, and my outlook on the various seasons of my life in ways too numerous to detail here. My prayer is that they will speak to your spirit and assist you in making greater strides in your life even on the days that you face another crossroad! The crossroads will be there. They come to press us to "greater things" where our destiny lies. God will not be satisfied with us trying to settle in the land of mediocrity! As Mahalia Jackson sang for us way back in the day, "You Have Got to Move!"

The movement through our various seasons will go smoother when we gather ourselves a community of sista-girls for support. We cannot journey alone! "Each of us is guided while we act as guides to one another, throughout the day, throughout our lives. We are interdependent. Everywhere we look, someone is learning from us and we from her. We often know not what we give, when we give it. And we seldom realize the value of what we're receiving at the time we accept it.

Resistance to what another person is offering us may be our natural response. But the passage of time highlights the value of the (sista) experience. We can look for comforters in our lives. They are there offering us strength and hope enough to see us through any difficulty.

"We need both the rough times (changing seasons) and the soft shoulders of our friends. They contribute equally to the designs our lives are weaving. The rough times press us to pray, to reach out to one another for solace. Our pain gives others the chance to heal our wounds. We are all healers offering strength. And we all need healing!"[4]

A CONTEMPORARY RUTH

Truly, I know this journey of Ruth and Naomi on a real personal level. Been there. Done that! And I continue to learn new lessons with each passing season. I could not make it without my sista-friends. I have so many, too many to name. As a pastor, I have a pastor. She is an African American Baptist pastor, Rev. Dr. Eleanor L. Miller. I met this tall and regal woman in seminary. We bonded and began a journey that continues over the miles and the years.

Eleanor has never left the Baptist denomination. She was born and raised in it, with a father who was a pastor and a mother who was an awesome "evangelist" and "first lady" of her husband's church. Eleanor is one of three sisters and a brother born to the Miller household. She has excelled as an Employee Assistance Personnel Officer (EAP) in a suburban hospital. She does private counseling with a specialty in substance abuse issues and with clergy colleagues. She is an author and an excellent preacher and teacher. She is a good sister to have on the journey.

One of her great gifts is that of confrontation and encouraging. That's sort of a backhand slap with a quick hug! She will challenge me on an issue but quickly point out just why she "knows" that I can do better or differently from our history. She is a great woman of fasting and prayer. I have spent the night and heard her praying in those wee hours unto a "hearing" God. I used to depend upon my mother to pray for me at all times. But Mama went home to be with God after I met Eleanor. Now, I depend upon Eleanor to pray when I have difficulty getting a prayer through. I just know that she does.

This woman of God has faced her own sets of circumstances over the years. She's never married or had children. She longs for her Boaz too. But she took over the church that her father established and was pastor of at his death. Now she has many "children."

She's a daughter of excellence. She was the one always there for her father as he walked through cancer and its attending ailments and treatments. Now, her mother, Ora, is undergoing dialysis treatments and Eleanor is also her driver and attendant.

Many look on this tall and stalwart woman as "strong and capable." And she is just that. But I'm also aware that she needs a sister on the journey and many of us are there just for her.

As a good sista, she dares to challenge me when I'm wrong. She supports my "six impossible imaginings" before breakfast! She helps me to clarify what God is saying in my life. She does confront me when I'm in my pity-pot modes. And, she will surely collaborate with Mista Chuck and I to do the "never been done before" things! And, she's always there to celebrate my joys.

A pastoral counselor of great wisdom and compassion, Eleanor offers both to all on her journey. A traveling "evangelist," she does a yearly "command and repeat" performance for several churches across the country. She's so at home with God's Word. She's able to put folks at ease with her soft-spoken approach, until she's disarming. She's a first on many levels because she dares to risk stepping out of her comfort zone. There are few folks that I allow to "pull my chains" or to call a halt to some of my foolishness. However, "Bishop" Miller fits in this category. For we have been on the journey to Wonderful, together, for such a long time.

We have celebrated each other's achievements. And, we have cried at each other's grief and pain. We pray for one another. We share several sista-friends and have spent vacation time, both being challenged and refreshed along our journey. We visit each other's home and I send her cards. She calls early in the morning to set me in order and to offer counsel and prayer. On my last visit to see her new home, I left with piles of her clothes that she gifted me with by surprise. She's an awesome dresser! So, leaving with her "closet cleaning" clothes was a real blessing. She's that sort of generous woman and that kind of sista-friend.

If Eleanor is my "bookend" on one side, there is Rev. Vera Jo Edington, an Anglo sista-friend, on my other side. I met Vera Jo in the days prior to my attending seminary. We met at a United Methodist School of Christian Mission in North Indiana. One of my African American girlfriends, a pastor's wife, had told me of her experiences at the campgrounds, so, I went, very defensively. The camp required that forty-eight women sleep in a dorm room and cook and eat in a common kitchen. It was a disaster waiting to happen!

One day, while preparing food in the common kitchen, one of the older white women asked me an offensive question about "colored people." I hit the roof! Most of the women in the kitchen felt that I had come down too hard on this older woman. Vera Jo came to my defense! She went against the mood of the majority and crossed over to begin a journey with this woman of color. Our relationship was on and has been ever since.

Vera Jo is one of the most dedicated Christian educators that I have ever encountered. She was working at First United Methodist Church, Hammond, Indiana, when we met, doing all sorts of creative things for all ages. Vicariously she went to seminary with me. She and her spouse, John, gave me some pumpkin colored drapes that hung in our first apartment. She would come to take me to lunch, a seminarian with little "free" funds. And she was my most persistent encourager. She, John, and another Anglo couple, Lynn Calvert and her now ex-husband, United Methodists from Iowa, were there for my graduation.

This was a significant event for many reasons. But, as my mother died the week before my graduation, these folks became my family. It's a small world after all! Vera Jo and John gave me a stole that was made of the same cloth that our first female bishop, Marge Matthews, had for her consecration. Although it's been years since I robed consistently, it remains one of my prized possessions.

When I was assigned pastor of my first African American congregation, Vera Jo came to work for me as the administrative assistant. It was an interesting period. For the congregation was not ready for a white woman and her spouse, who joined too!

Vera Jo began a program, Discovery: Unlimited as an after school tutorial. It took off and involved many different people to make it a success. Then, she decided to make her position formal by enrolling in seminary.

Vera Jo graduated from Garrett-Evangelical Theological Seminary and went on to be ordained as a Diaconal Minister of Christian Education. It was a rich moment in history. She worked at the Olympia Fields UMC, where she was allowed to serve as co-pastor when the senior pastor had health complications. She was so loved and very well received, for she's a blessing to have on a journey with you.

This is another sista-friend, and her husband, John, is my brother. We have stayed at each other's home, eaten and broken bread together, and shared in the drama's of our children and grandchildren. We have presented some of the most creative ministry opportunities for those who were serious about growing in their faith journey. I never knew at that School of Christian Missions that Vera Jo and I were entering a life journey. It's all been wonderful. Vera has had health challenges that began with a stroke after knee surgery. She continues her ministry of calling, cards, and e-mails to keep contact during even her hospitalizations. I ask you to join me in holding her and John in prayers.

Eleanor and Vera Jo are only two of my many sista-friends who dare journey with me via visits, phone calls, e-mails, and faxes. They send me money to sustain the ministries of WomanSpace: A Sacred Space for God's Bodacious Professional Women. They mail me butterflies from themselves and from their friends! They send me tapes, CDs, butterfly flags, and other signs of tangible love to keep me lifted when a season has me in its death hold.

My sista-friends dare to write books, poems, sermons, and daily devotional "bytes" to encourage my spirit. I am sheltered under the love of many awesome sisters on the journey.

When I had "left" the United Methodist denomination— never officially, but emotionally, spiritually, and mentally—God had a group of United Methodist Women from West Alabama to call and ask me to come and be the principle preacher for their annual Spiritual Formation Weekend.

I made the price high so that they could not afford me! I didn't want to be bothered with anyone United Methodist. I had been hurt by the denomination and never intended to have any dealings with them in person again. But God called a shift in my journey! The African American president of this group of primarily Anglo women knew one of my good friends, in her hometown. So President Mattie Battle got my sista-friend, Dr. Janette Kotey, minister of music at Huntsville First Baptist Church, to call me. Well, when Janette called me there was no question that I'd not talk with Mattie.

Mattie called and we fell in love over the phone. The national United Methodist Women had put my book *Jesus and Those Bodacious Women* on their reading list. Many of the women had read the work and wanted to meet me, hear me tell the stories, and experience me in worship. Sista Mattie told me to expect a call from the director of programs, Mrs. Pattie Perry Finney.

Talk about a whirlwind! Pattie called me. Pattie e-mailed me. Pattie "snail mailed" me. And Pattie hooked me into coming to journey with the group. She gave me some instructions of their needs. She asked me how I would like the time to be used. We became sista-friends just by trying to make a weekend event extraordinary for our sisters! I went to teach. I was loved into a new, better, and different journey with "our" denomination.

The time in West Alabama changed and revolutionized my life! The loving acceptance of this group of women, who were and are my sisters, overwhelmed me. They loved me. They welcomed me. They accepted me. They affirmed me. They apologized to me on behalf of those who had hurt me within the denomination. They inquired of my well-being and my intentions for my journey. And we went on a journey together that allowed me to "see" a more grand vision of the church than I had experienced prior. I left there refreshed, renewed, and relieved that both the United Methodist Church and myself had grown!

The seasons come and go. The seasons change and pass. The seasons call us to move through them and to endure the lessons and the blessings that they come to bring. Each season arrives with both the known and the unknown qualities that make life both interesting and challenging. It is the way of life. And the

God of every season makes it a habit to put sisters and sista-friends in our path to help us make successful journeys.

My sister, Riene, is in her own apartment now. It's surely a new season for each of us as we adjust again. The issues of life shifted and her former home was no longer a place where she could live, so we invited her to come and spend time with us. I had told her that her response as she traveled this health-challenging journey was to be, "I'm on my way to Wonderful." Little did I realize that our home would be her "Wonderful" for a season. After a year, the season changed again, and Riene was able to move into her own place. Thanks be to God! God is faithful and so are we.

I have read and reread the words of Isaiah 66:11–13 from the New Jerusalem Bible as we continue our journey through another season of our lives. I share them with you:

> May you be sucked and satisfied from the consoling breast of God.
> May you drink deep and with delight from God's generous nipple.
> May you be suckled, carried on God's hip, and fondled in her lap.
> As a mother comforts a child, so shall I comfort you, says God.

We're off, not to see the Wizard of Oz, but to see all of the side trips that we will be led on as we now journey together to Wonderful! I'm set in my ways, and so is Riene. I like having things done my way, and so does Riene. I'm not the most organized individual, but Riene is so well organized. I'm a person who enjoys nature and Riene does not. I can easily go to bed with the chickens and Riene likes to do "busy" work at night, "while it's quiet," she says! Whatever I do, she questions. Whatever she does, I question. But, the journey to Wonderful was on! My next book might have to detail our journey! We love each other better when we live separately.

Thanks for taking this journey through the covenant of Ruth to Naomi with me. I appreciate sharing with you. Don't hesitate to drop me a line at wtwmi99@aol.com and let me know what you think of my observations. I look so forward to hearing from you. I pray that you have all my other books, written with YOU in mind!

I ask your prayers as we journey to Wonderful. Please be advised that I am certainly praying for YOU! Let me remind you that the Source of Being is above and within us.

The source of being is above,
Who gives life to all people;
For people are satisfied, and do not die of famine,
For God gives them life,
That they may live prosperously
on the earth and not die of famine.

—A prayer from the Zulu, South Africa[5]

I pray for each of us, that the God of the Ages opens our hearts to greater seasons of imaginations, opens our minds to greater visions of our destiny, and opens our spirits to encompass what God desires for us.

I encourage you to read the entire book of Ruth before you call a group of women to study it together. Then prepare yourself for great movement in the Spirit. We have each other. A wall plaque I've seen says this: "We have God for us. We have Jesus with us. We have the Holy Spirit in us and all of heaven's angels are on our side! (Roy Lessin)."

That's good enough to make our journey great! Shalom, Dear One! God's best shalom!

LET'S PAUSE AND BREATHE!

1. What season are you in currently?
2. Who are the "bookends" that you have in place to help you through?
3. Who is the "Boaz" in your life? (This does not have to be a romantic entanglement!)
4. Who was the last person that you took a journey with who left you hanging?
5. What did you learn from that experience?
6. What have you learned about the Christian year and its seasons that will help you along your journey?
7. Are you Ruth or Naomi today?
8. If Naomi, what's your new name? _____
9. If Ruth, what's the name of your new "infant"? _____

10. What was your greatest lesson from this book? I will always remember that:

_____

_____

_____

_____

_____

_____

_____

_____

APPENDIX

This work is about the decisions that women are often forced to make; about facing a crossroad and having to choose new options; about feeling as if the past has cheated you and that the future holds no promise. It's about how women deal with issues of crosscultural relationships, interethnic marriages, difficult times, and leaving the familiar for the unknown. It's about leadership strategies that women develop in order to live and to survive, about a journey into the world of risk, possible rejection, and perhaps even death as a possible consequence. Yet this work is a love story that has withstood the tests of time.

Following are suggestions for leading a small-group study using this book. A ten-week time period would be ideal, one week per chapter, with a week prior to become acquainted with the other women and the material.

On the first week have women covenant that they will have read and digested the required materials by the group's gathering. This will save time and energy if all are on the same pages, knowing the same things, and ready to share their insights. Another requirement is a covenant to keep all information within your group, not sharing another woman's "issues" with even spouses or significant others.

The opening question might pertain to the title: "How do we know when it's time for a new journey?" This book is about three women who had met a serious time of suffering together. They had survived. But one day the senior woman decided, "It's time for a change!" How do we come to this major step in our lives? What are some of the signs that call out, "Change time"?

PRAYER: God, what used to hold me "here" is not working. What used to satisfy me no longer does. The days of uncertainty and nonclarity are gone. My inner cup is empty. My capacity to "hold on" has fled. I need more satisfaction. I require more of life, and I demand more out of me. I'm here, at the crossroad. I know what's behind me. The former attraction has faded and what it meant I can't even remember. The future is murky and you have not provided a roadmap for me. Yet, Woman Wisdom, the intuition that stirs within, the unrest that is alive and moving, says it's time for me to make a change. "Go" is in my spirit. "Move" is twinkling in my toes. "Leave" is ringing in my head. Right now, "where" does not matter. All that I do know is that I'm out of here!

Ask each woman to write out her own answer to the following statement: God, I hear you calling me to go and to do _____

_____.

The beginning of our journey together demands that we come to an agreement about the word "love." Ask the women in the group to come up with a common definition that will be the standard during your time together through this work.

A good place to start is with the three Greek words that address the one English word "love." Explain the meaning of eros, familia, and agape. Spend some time refecting as a group on the various times that women have been deceived by false use of the word "love."

The dynamics of muticultural relationships are not new. In this story we find a loving relationship between two women of different backgrounds, cultures, religions, and ethnic groups. There is a book on the market entitled My First White Friend. It might be a reference point for this group to talk about that time in life when they chose a friend who was "different." Several television shows feature relationships that survive the years with women of different ethnic groups. A snippet of one of them could be a lead-in to conversation.

Both of these "starring" women had to wrestle with the issue of being "accepted" by a strange country and a strange people with strange customs. Address this frightening stage of life and allow others to talk about their personal development in this area. There is always the fear of rejection. What are common tips for "fitting in" when with strangers? Share the fear experienced during transition periods in our lives.

The dynamic of female leadership is strong in this book. Address the fact that Ruth and Esther are the only two books about women that made it into the biblical canon. What characteristics for leadership are essential for women?

This is another time that a common definition—of "leadership"—might be helpful. There are three distinct principles of leadership set forth: 1) Step up to the plate, 2) have a firm/sure foundation, and 3) make sure/firm decisions.

How have these principles been acted out in the life of women in the group? What is required of a woman to "step up?" When can one be sure that one's foundation is secure? Who has been a female role model who made "sure" decisions? Are real leaders born or created by the situations that life presents?

PRAYER: *Gracious God, I'm simply trying to make it day by day. I'm doing all that I can to hold it together. My aspirations have not included stepping out, stepping on, and surely not stepping into a leadership role. I know that I can maintain. I know how to sustain. I can even refrain. But lead? My brothers were taught to lead. My brothers were told to be in charge. My brothers were raised to be out front. As a girl, I was to be quiet, to be hidden and to not know much of anything. My intellect was not respected. My opinion was not sought. My words were not heeded. So I learned to be a background individual. I learned how to be subtle. I learned how to work around obstacles without showing any leadership skills. Now are you pushing me to the front? Is this really you, God, calling me to be in charge and to lead? Yes, I know about Ruth and Esther. Of course I remember Deborah and Hannah too. But I'm a different sort of woman. Or am I?*

Ask each woman to write out her answer to the following: God, I sense you saying that I need to take the lead in _____

_____.

One of the common issues among women is that of gathering, holding, and cluttering up our space. We hold onto "old" stuff, and even people, when they have passed their season of goodwill and productivity in our lives. Ask women to name ten items from either their home or closets they could get rid of and never miss. Share the discoveries.

Now ask them to name five people in their lives who need to be cleared out of their space. Remind them that people come into our lives for either a season or a reason. Too many of us are holding on to folks who are dragging us backwards and keeping us stuck in "yesterday." Give them about three minutes for silent reflection. Ask them to put check marks by the ones that they are fully aware have passed both their season and reason.

When we begin a journey to Wonderful, everyone cannot go with us! There are many persons who don't want to leave the mess that they are in, and they don't want us to get unstuck either! Yet, in order to embrace the new journey to Wonderful, some old stuff—and people—need to be shed. One of the "old" things that women need to visit are the limiting habits that they have come to accept as "truth." Ask the women to begin to name some of the learned habits that make our lives unbearable and now need to be shed.

This book is about the bonding relationship between two women of different generations, ethnic groups, and cultures. They were forced to become a team. On the journey to Wonderful we all need companions who have our back. What kind of team members do we need on our new journey?

Facing stressful situations, like Naomi, we too, will make poor decisions. What has making bad choices taught us? It might have been a wrong move; however, every lesson learned helps us to grow. How can we make better, life-giving choices and decisions?

Severe depression is not new to women. Naming depression is what is more recent. Too many women have chosen to have a nervous breakdown or to commit suicide when faced with the difficulties of life. Have the women talk about the "walking mental breakdowns" they have experienced. It's a much better option than suicide!

PRAYER: *Voices! Voices! Voices! God, there are too many voices! Ancient voices echo in my mind, setting my limits and choices. The voices of my elders are so strong and I don't want to displease them or have them feel that their ways are not good enough for me today.*

Choices! Choices! Choices! The world is offering too many choices! There seems to be no limits and moral bankruptcy is the voice of today. Where is the voice of the Church? Where is the voice of the community? I cannot speak for all and I cannot remain silent any longer!

Decisions! Decisions! Decisions! God, you are awaiting my decision! The journey to Wonderful lies before me and there is sorting that I must do. I must choose between what is good and what is your best for me! Spirit of the Living God, I need to hear, with certainty, your voice! Speak, God! This servant is listening with a brand new attitude!

Ask the women to fill in the blank: I hear the Holy Spirit calling me to leave behind _____.

Well, my beloved sisters, we're off on another trip; this time our destination is Wonderful! I'm praying for our journey. I'm ready to arrive! But, as usual, I know that our travel requires time. Please write me and let me know about your journey. Please keep me in prayer as I travel too. Remember that I'll travel to your destination and for awhile we can journey together! My email and website addresses are: wtwmi99@aol.com and www.geocities.com/womanspace2003.

ENDNOTES

PREFACE

1. Amy-Jill Levine, "Ruth," *The Women's Bible Commentary*, ed. Carol A. Newsom and Sharon H. Ringe (Louisville: Westminister John Knox Press, 1992), 78.

2. Phenessa A. Grey, "I'm Through Crying," from *My Soul's Surrender* (Portland, Ore.: First Books, 2002), 3. Copyright © 2000, 2002. Reprinted with permission.

INTRODUCTION

1. Paul Harvey, nationally syndicated radio show.

CHAPTER 1

1. Angela Mitchell and Kennise Herring, *What the Blues Is All About* (New York: Perigee Books, 1998), 7.

2. Amy-Jill Levine, "Ruth," *The Women's Bible Commentary*, ed. Carol A. Newsom and Sharon H. Ringe (Louisville: Westminster John Knox Press, 1992), 80.

3. Zora Neale Hurston, *Dust Tracks on a Road* (New York: HarperCollins, 1965), 42.

CHAPTER 2

1. Cheryl Forbes, *Imagination: Embracing a Theology of Wonder* (Portland, Ore: Multnomah Press, 1986), 19–25.
2. Ibid., 75
3. Ibid., 74.
4. Ibid., 74.

CHAPTER 3

1. Cheryl Townsend Gilkes, *If It Wasn't for the Woman* (New York: Orbis Books, 2001), 7–8.
2. Lucie E. Campbell (1885–1963), "Something Within," 1919 (*The African American Heritage Hymnal*, 493).

CHAPTER 4

1. Robert Solow, *Work and Welfare* (Princeton: N.J.: Princeton University Press, 1998).
2. Rebecca Blank, *It Takes a Nation* (Princeton: N.J.: Princeton University Press, 1998).
3. Jack Patterson, *Four Blind Mice* (New York: Little Brown and Company, 2001).

CHAPTER 5

1. Phillip Eastman, *Are You My Mother?* (New York: Random House, 1960).
2. Jill Nelson, *Straight, No Chaser!* (New York: Penquin Books, 1997), 4–5.
3. Ibid., 99.
4. Lucie E. Campbell (1885–1963), "Something Within," 1919 (*The African American Heritage Hymnal*, 493).

CHAPTER 6

1. Brenda Lane Richardson and Dr. Brenda Wade, *What Mama Couldn't Tell Us about Love* (New York: HarperCollins, 1999), 22–27.
2. Ibid., 27.

CHAPTER 7

1. Sheron Patterson, *New Faith: A Black Woman's Guide to Reformation, Re-Creation, Rediscovery, Renaissance, Resurrection, and Revival* (Minneapolis: Fortress Press, 2000), 66.
2. Ibid.
3. Ibid., 67.

CHAPTER 8

1. Theresa L. Fry Brown, *God Don't Like Ugly: African American Women Handing on Spiritual Values* (Nashville: Abingdon Press, 2001), 36.
2. Ibid.
3. Ibid., 37.
4. Herbert Lockyer, *All the Women of the Bible* (Grand Rapids: Zondervan Books, 1988), 148.

CHAPTER 9

1. Amy-Jill Levine, "Ruth," *The Women's Bible Commentary*, ed. Carol A. Newsom and Sharon H. Ringe (Louisville: Westminster John Knox Press, 1992), 84.
2. Dorothy Bryant, quoted in Karen Casey, *Each Day a New Beginning: A Meditation Book and Journal for Daily Reflection* (Center City, Minn.: Hazelden Publishing & Educational Services, 2001), Jan 3.
3. Karen Casey, *Each Day a New Beginning: A Meditation Book and Journal for Daily Reflection* (Center City, Minn.: Hazelden Publishing & Educational Services, 2001), Jan 3.
4. Karen Casey, *Each Day a New Beginning: A Meditation Book and Journal for Daily Reflection* (Center City, Minn.: Hazelden Publishing & Educational Services, 2001), Feb. 1.
5. Bishop Desmond Tutu, *The African Prayer Book* (New York: Doubleday Books, 1995), 16.

BIBLIOGRAPHY

Brown, Theresa L. Fry. *God Don't Like Ugly: African American Women Handing on Spiritual Values.* Nashville: Abingdon Press, 2001.

Casey, Karen. *Each Day a New Beginning: A Meditation Book and Journal for Daily Reflection.* Center City, Minn.: Hazelden Publishing & Educational Services, 2001.

Forbes, Cheryl. *Imagination: Embracing a Theology of Wonder.* Portland, Ore.: Multnomah Press, 1986.

Gilkes, Cheryl Townsend. *If It Wasn't for the Woman.* New York: Orbis Books, 2001.

Grey, Phenessa A. *My Soul's Surrender.* Portland, Ore.: First Books, 2002.

Hollies, Linda H. *Jesus and Those Bodacious Women.* Cleveland: Pilgrim Press, 1997.

Lockyer, Herbert. *All the Women of the Bible.* Grand Rapids: Zondervan Publishing, 1988.

Mitchell, Angela, and Kennise Herring, *What the Blues Is All About.* New York: Perigee Books, 1998.

Newsom, Carol A., and Sharon H. Ringe, eds. *The Women's Bible Commentary.* Louisville: Westminster John Knox Press, 1992.

Patterson, Sheron. *New Faith: A Black Woman's Guide to Reformation, Re-Creation, Rediscovery, Renaissance, Resurrection, and Revival.* Minneapolis: Fortress Press, 2000.

Ruth and Esther: Shepherd Notes. Nashville: Broadman & Holman Publishers, 1973.

Richards, Lawrence O. *The Bible Readers' Companion.* Owings Mill, Md.: Halo Press, 1991.

Richardson, Brenda Lane, and Dr. Brenda Wade. *What Mama Couldn't Tell Us about Love.* New York: Harper Collins, 1999.

Spence, H. D. M., and Joseph S. Exell. *The Pulpit Commentary, Volume 4, Ruth, I & II Samuel.* Grand Rapids: William B. Eerdmans, 1976.

Tutu, Bishop Desmond. *The African Prayer Book.* New York: Doubleday, 1995.

Williams, Michael E., ed. *The Storyteller's Companion to the Bible.* Nashville: Abingdon Press, 1993.